KILLER
Stories

KILLER Stories

Conversations with
South African serial murderers

BRIN HODGSKISS

and Nicole Engelbrecht

Jonathan Ball Publishers
JOHANNESBURG · CAPE TOWN

Originally published in South Africa in 2024 by
JONATHAN BALL PUBLISHERS
A division of Media24 (Pty) Ltd
PO Box 33977
Jeppestown
2043

ISBN 978-1-77619-332-5
ebook ISBN 978-1-77619-333-2
audiobook ISBN 978-1-77619-434-6

www.jonathanball.co.za
www.x.com/JonathanBallPub
www.facebook.com/JonathanBallPublishers

Cover by Rudi Louw
Design and typesetting by Martine Barker
Set in Arno Pro and Acumin Variable Concept

Printed by **novus print**, a division of Novus Holdings

This book is dedicated to preserving an idea –
the idea that listening to one another's stories
can make life better.

Contents

Introduction

It all started standing over the body of a dead schoolgirl. Her throat had been cut from ear to ear, and she was sprawled naked on her back.

It's funny how memory plays tricks on you. I can't remember the colours of the bricks that made up the low building we were standing in. Were they yellow, or the usual municipal red? Were the medical examiner's scrubs pale green or light blue, or some other colour?

What I can remember are the tiny traces of the girl's last moments, vivid as flashbulbs. Her grazed knees. The little bits of veld grass sticking to her hair. The sickening wobble of her neck as the examiner checked it. 'Ah, yes, it is broken,' he confirmed. 'It can easily happen when all the supporting muscles are cut through.'

This was in Grahamstown (now Makhanda) in the late 1990s. I was part of an academic team from Rhodes University supporting the police with offender profiling on active cases. The building we were in was the medical examiner's office for the policing district, just behind the police station. Both stood guard near the top of the broad road that, in my memory, marked the point where the tides of the old student town met those of the township. The road had originally been built wide to accommodate the turning of ox wagons. Now it was bubbling with the usual mix of people and traffic and livestock that own the streets of Eastern Cape towns.

I remember walking up and down that street a few times over those months, blowing the greasy mortuary smell out of my nostrils, feeling slightly dizzy at being surrounded by the living.

Our small team usually went in on the same day as the weekly intake of murder victims from across the policing district: a span of rural settlements and towns in rolling scrubby hills. Usually, the dead in the room outnumbered the living.

On that day, our team of trainee psychologists was in the mortuary to start the process of creating an offender profile. That meant we were trying, from the characteristics of the crime, to infer the nature of the offender. In the traces left on the schoolgirl's body, we hoped to discover more about the mind of the man who had murdered her. These inferences would form another strand in the net of evidence and intelligence that the police wove to convict a killer.

I can't remember the details of what we inferred in our eventual profile. I wouldn't be able to say, with absolute clarity, whether the thread we contributed to the police net was useful when the man was arrested. What I remember more vividly than anything was the rush of emotion standing over the dead girl, an incredible surge of outrage, exhilaration and purpose: this is something I have to do something about; I can help to stop this from happening again.

It was that torrent of emotion – or the memory of it – that carried me into my 15-year career in policing.

The desire to apply psychology to solve real-life problems remains with me. The first thing that burst of emotion motivated me to do, though, was to volunteer to help the South African Police Service (SAPS) expand its database of information on serial murderers. That's what I did over the next two years, travelling around between maximum-security prisons, speaking to men who had committed serial murder. I spoke to a dozen in total.

As I went from prison to prison, it became clear that the stories I was being told were important. The men I spoke to wanted to tell their stories; it was important to them that they were heard. And as I spoke with convicted murderers about crime after crime, their narratives began revealing a darker aspect: they had helped to create their offending.

◆

In 2007, I was working in England with a fellow intelligence analyst called Mark. It was a sunny day and we were standing in a field, doing the ABC of serious investigation: assume nothing; believe nothing; check everything. In particular, we were checking everything.

It was the early days of a murder inquiry and we were sorting through a deluge of information. Usually, the first hours after a murder are the 'golden' ones: high value, with the decisions made then rippling through the investigation afterwards.

This deluge was different. In this case, the death had happened some time before.

In December 2006, a baby had died. Her name was Leeya. She was at home with her parents and her older sister. It was bath time. Suddenly she stopped breathing. A panicked call to the emergency services followed, 999 operators talking the parents through how they could resuscitate their daughter, paramedics bursting through the front door to take over and rush her to hospital.

Leeya's life-support machine was turned off 12 days later.

Over those 12 days, medical staff had become suspicious. Injuries to her nose and fingers were unusual. The postmortem revealed Leeya had suffered 22 broken ribs, a fractured skull and a fractured thigh: severe force had been applied to her right leg. She had also been bitten and shaken hard. Some of her injuries were old, some newer, suggesting she had been hurt over a period of time; the judge at her eventual trial would comment that 'when she was not asleep, Leeya must have been in excruciating pain'.

She had come (in the words of the court document) into 'forceful contact with something hard' at least once – what this meant was, in the opinion of the investigation team, smacking her soft skull into a bath tap on that final, fatal day.

Mark and I were part of the Cambridgeshire Constabulary's major investigation team, which rolled into action for serious and complex investigations, usually murders. We were in a prefabricated hut built on the edge of the police headquarters' sports field; the hut had been thrown up in a hurry to accommodate a high-profile case some years previously. We were on a deadline. There is a time limit for how long you can hold someone in police custody before you charge them with a crime, and we were racing against that clock.

As intelligence analysts, our task was to create order in the wave of information flooding in, trying to find enough evidence to make a charge stick. Information comes from many sources: statements from suspects, doctors, officers and witnesses, telephone records, audio and video recordings, and so on – all of which need to be woven together to create the story of the crime. You never know if you're going to find anything when you start. We just have to slog through, step by step, line by line, doing the detail, checking everything, as fast as we can.

Analysts usually start by creating a timeline: what happened, when, and to whom.

Mark and I were creating a very specific timeline – or, rather, three timelines, side by side – comparing the transcripts of the 999 operator call with the statements made by the Leeya's mother and father when they were arrested and interviewed. For speed and in the spirit of our makeshift accommodation, Mark and I had abandoned the specialist mapping software we'd usually use and rescued a whiteboard that someone had thrown into the bins behind HQ, teaming up to hand-draw a timeline more quickly: black and green marker pens for what the dead child's parents had said and done; blue marker pen to chart what the 999 recording had heard them doing.

We'd completed the interview with the parents and written down the key events side by side. They described everything you would expect young parents to do, faced with a baby suddenly stopping breathing at bath time: the screams, the rushing together, calling 999, carrying the baby downstairs so the 999 operator could direct them in administering first aid, the lengthy attempts at resuscitation (interspersed by trips to fetch equipment, call more help, get clothing for an imminent trip to hospital), the eventual panicked lament that the baby was dead. We found some discrepancies, but nothing major, nothing you couldn't put down to trauma, the hectic confusion of your young child collapsing in your arms.

Mark was now reading out the 999 transcript. I was writing on the board.

'Stop skipping forward,' I snapped.

'What?' asked Mark.

'Just read what's on the bloody page.'

'I am! That's what it says.'

I looked from Mark, to board, to transcript. But how could it? It didn't match the parents' stories at all. It missed a huge chunk of their interview accounts: all the details of their rescue efforts, resuscitating the floppy Leeya, panicked … Oh!

It clicked into place in my mind. There was no way they could have done everything they said they had done. They had lied. Got them!

The author Thomas Harris says in *Silence of the Lambs*, 'Problem solving is a savage art, and we are born to it.' There is something savage in the sense of triumph when a piece of the puzzle falls into place, trapping someone who has done wrong. Leeya's parents were charged with causing the death of their child and, in 2009, mother and father were sentenced to 16 years and five years in prison, respectively.

While the charge and eventual convictions weren't down to our analysis alone, writing the stories down and comparing them side by side had helped the investigating team to see patterns that might otherwise have been missed. (Yes, I apologised to the enthusiastic and ever-polite Mark, too.)

This echoed what I did to prepare for each interview with a serial murderer. Each interview I conducted was the end point of months of preparation, each a mini-investigation in its own right. It started with finding the people to talk to, usually by driving to Pretoria in my second-hand Volkswagen Jetta, to the office block housing the Investigative Psychology Unit of the SAPS. I'd head through the iron gates at the entrance, up to their office at the front of the building. There I would perch, copying dockets on a spare wood-laminate table, checking media reports and summaries, gathering the information I would need to find and speak to the serial murderers I wanted to study.

Initial research complete, I would contact the investigating officers, many of whom had been trained by the Investigative Psychology Unit. I wanted their insight into the men they had captured. Sometimes I would visit them in their offices, sometimes chat over the phone and, on one memorable occasion, catch five minutes with a legendary South African detective during an intermission in the trial of one of the men he had caught. They were all different, but all helpful and courteous.

Last of all, I set about tracking down where the offender had landed up in the prison system. Correctional Services had given permission for my research and were, like all the public servants I met, unfailingly helpful. It still took many phone calls, and a few false starts, to find out where each of the men I wanted to speak to was held. They could be sent to one prison while awaiting trial, then another once convicted, then a third as their sentence progressed (or as they were considered more or less dangerous), then a fourth to be closer to their support networks outside prison, if they were fortunate enough to have any, and so on. This made finding someone difficult.

Sometimes, when I found them, there would be another conversation with a prison psychologist, creating another layer of knowledge.

The result of this searching and collecting was that by the time I pulled up outside a prison, I knew something of the man waiting for me and what he had done: a skeleton timeline of his life, crimes, and what others thought of him.

In almost all my interviews, perched between us on a table, or balanced on a chair an electrical cord's distance from the nearest plug, was the silent whirring witness of my tape recorder. The stack of audio tapes, at least four hours per interview, were then carefully labelled and stacked at the end of each of day's work. Each evening, usually sitting at my parents' old yellowwood dining-room table, I made notes of my feelings and impressions, and questions to ask for the next day's interviews. Tapes, interview questionnaires and notes were all then packed into a suitcase for transportation back to university.

Just over four years after the interviews, I opened that suitcase again, intent on studying for a PhD. I wanted to delve deep into the interview tapes and find out how the stories the men told about themselves were reflected in the crimes they had committed. I hoped this knowledge would better help us to catch them.

Perhaps I had imagined that, simply by listening to them talk, the meaning in their stories would immediately be obvious. If I listened hard and deep enough, I thought, the meaning would be found like a golden thread running through their words. So, I found myself, at nights after work, doing the same thing as I had done during the day when I had made timelines as an intelligence analyst.

When we talk, our ideas pour out of us in a torrent, or leak out in drips, or leap from event to event like a frog jumping between puddles. We may jump backwards and forwards through time with a single word. We hesitate, repeat ourselves, lose our way and loop back. We avoid the point and reveal what matters only by implication and association. It takes work to smooth that into the cause and effect of a story, marching in one direction through time. It's more work to discern the key characters, to link them to the key themes, and to shape an interpretation about what it all means.

Even then, you can miss something. I missed a big something, which I noticed only ten years later when I started to write this book. In many of my interviews with serial murderers, I noted things like 'It was difficult to understand the chronology of events', 'He struggled to express himself' or 'The meaning wasn't immediately apparent'. The men's accounts seemed to be cloaked in a fog: vague, with events and emotions and motivations drifting in and out of view.

Writing my PhD, I wondered if this was my fault. I questioned my linguistic ability in Afrikaans, fretted over my interview structure, doubted my skill as an interviewer. I was digging for the deeper meaning in their words, frustrated that it was so difficult to draw it out.

Just like with Mark in front of the whiteboard, I realised the truth only when I looked at a couple of the cases side by side: the fog was itself a pattern. The confusion about their inner story, the seeming lack of coherence and meaning, was significant. One interviewee even acknowledged this, observing that the interview was a chance for him to make sense of his inner world: 'It's an education for me,' he said; 'I am bettering myself.' His interview was peppered with moments of befuddled introspection as he worked through the meaning of his actions: 'I could have felt this, but I'm not sure', 'I may have thought this, I can't say, really', 'I don't think I enjoyed it, but [the psychologist] said I did, otherwise I wouldn't have killed again, so maybe it was so'. This confusion and ambiguity seemed incongruous at the heart of someone whose crimes seemed so confident and decisive, and it meant his story took many readings to understand.

Other interviewees expressed similar confusion. One said, 'The thing is … I think back to the crimes a lot. I ask myself. I try to find answers. I ask myself, "What happened that night? What the hell happened there? What was wrong with me?" I ask myself sometimes, "Why didn't I walk away?"' When confronted by his inability to make sense of his own story, this murderer kept looping back to the influence of circumstance, of his co-perpetrator, of occult powers overwhelming him.

Would it be possible to be blind to more? I wondered this when my notes threw up a contradiction between what a man said in our interview and what a crime scene report, a court document or a witness had said. Was the man simply lying? Was he saying what he believed to be true? How could you tell the difference?

We humans are very good at shaping the reality around us to fit what we believe, yet at the same time being blind to what is driving our behaviour.

◆

On another sunny afternoon, a decade after I had stood in that field with Mark doing our ABCs and almost 20 years after I had spoken to serial murderers, I decided to kill myself.

I knew how I would do it. I knew where I would do it. It was such a vivid image, accompanied by an amazing feeling of relief. I wouldn't have to feel this pain any more. The feeling of being a helpless failure would be gone. I would be at ease.

That feeling was immediately followed by intense anger. I pictured my then eight-year-old son walking into the garage and finding me. Violent death is ugly. How could I do that to him? Every death smashes through the lives of the living. How could I do that to my loved ones?

I was so angry at myself for letting things get that far that I spoke to someone. I found the first professional I could. I spoke and spoke, and I started to work out how I was going to find my way out of the trap I'd built for myself. For it was a self-built trap. It was a thousand small whispers: 'You failed in the police', 'You didn't protect your family', 'You let yourself down', 'Nothing you do makes any difference', 'Give it all up' … I had barely even noticed the voices.

Noticing them didn't make them go away, though. So began the process of finding ways out of my web of inner whispers and contradictory selves. One of the ways I found was stories.

One evening, a couple of months later, my son and I were sitting by an open window, waiting to watch a lunar eclipse. On an impulse, I started telling him a story I made up on the spot. It was a children's story in the style of African stories that my mom used to play on the cassette player in her car.

That first story was called 'The Rabbit and the Nightsnake'. I finished it and I expected my son would be bored. Instead, he said, 'Can you tell me another one?' So I made up another story. After that, he said, 'Can you tell me one more?' I said, 'Okay, but after this you need to get ready for bed.'

As I stood up, he gave me a huge hug and he said, 'Dad, I just love your stories. They make me want to cry; I love them so much.'

I thought, Well, I need to do more of that.

I started to look for more stories – not necessarily children's stories, but the type of stories I could tell myself to keep myself moving forward into the light. This meant I had to listen more openly to the stories other people were telling.

The more I shared my story with people, the more other people shared theirs in return. As I heard more stories, the more I realised that many, many other people have the same dark whispers. It was like the beginning of spring, when you start to see green shoots and discover that the more you look for them, the more green shoots you see.

The more I showed people my secret self, the more I understood that being undermined by our inner stories is not the sole preserve of serial murderers. It happens to all of us. If it could happen to someone like me, growing up surrounded by love and support, privileged in almost every sense of the word, then no one is safe. That is why I decided to write this book.

In Part I, my co-author Nicole Engelbrecht and I take you where most true-crime books stop: beyond the prison gates and into the minds of the men who committed these crimes, in their own words. In the killer stories that follow, we break each into two parts. The first part, written by Nicole, describes the crimes committed by the killers. The second part, written by me, takes you into the inner world of the serial murderer, in his own words. Each killer's story explores a different aspect of our internal narratives: the structure, the content, the themes or the characters. Each is written in the crimes it creates.

In Part II, I look more deeply at our psychology, the power stories have over our minds, and how we might turn them from harmful to helpful. And Part III shows the possibilities of stories.

◆

Storytelling is one of the most fundamental ways we humans make sense of ourselves and our world. Some of the stories we create to make sense of the world, though, have terrible consequences for ourselves and for others.

Each of the six 'killer stories' in this book is drawn from my experience of interviewing serial murderers in the year 2000, when I was in my early twenties and studying for my Master of Arts (MA) in psychology. Many of the interviews were conducted in Afrikaans, and I have translated the interviews into English.

Sometimes, though, when the English word doesn't truly capture the meaning of the original, I have also included the specific Afrikaans word used. The quotations throughout the book are taken from audio recordings made at the time or, sometimes, from handwritten notes I made during an interview. To make it easier to read I haven't used some of the conventions of academic quotations, such as the use of ellipsis to show when I've cut out unnecessary words. I was careful to preserve the meaning, though. The words are always the actual words the men used.

You might wonder if we've used the real names of any of the offenders or victims. We haven't, and we've also changed or concealed locations. We've done this to protect both the identity of the men who were interviewed and that of their victims. Certain ethical rules apply to any research in psychology in which human subjects are used. Those rules ensure that people are protected and that they don't suffer because of their participation in research. Before I interviewed any of the men, they signed a consent form that explained the purposes of the research, and that the material collected for the research may be used again. Specifically, it stated that should the material be used publicly, their anonymity would be protected. (Stefaans Coetzee is the exception: he was not part of the original academic research – he was interviewed recently, especially for this book – and he gave his consent to being identified.)

As the reader, you may feel the need to figure out the true identity of each offender. That, of course, is up to you. There's certainly no prize for guessing correctly. What I would recommend instead, though, is that you use that energy to immerse yourself fully in these stories. Let them speak to you. Listen to how these stories shaped the lives of other human beings, whatever their names.

Since we tell ourselves stories, we can fall prey to the same killer stories that undid the men I spoke to. Understand how stories can shape your life too.

Dr Brin Hodgskiss
2024

PART I
CONDEMNED

1 Kyle: The fog

The crimes

Although we, as a true-crime-consuming public, have set ideas about what 'standard' serial murderer behaviour looks like, it's important to remember that much of that is curated by American-produced television programmes. This is not to say it's inaccurate; it's just mostly accurate for American serial murderers.

As with most other types of crime, including single or one-off murders, serial murder and the criminology behind these crimes are shaped by the country in which they occur. Socioeconomic, political, religious and law-enforcement circumstances all affect the way in which serial murderers behave.

One of the most popular beliefs around serial murderers is that they frequently target sex workers. This statement holds true in the United States, where associate professor of criminal justice Kenna Quinet's 2011 study puts the number of sex-worker victims at 32 per cent of all female victims of serial murder. That number is only from solved cases, though. Of the ten unsolved series this same study looked at, 90 per cent of the victims were female sex workers.

Although many American serial murderers claim they targeted sex workers as vengeance for some or other perceived slight they endured by a member of that group (and some may be telling their

1

version of the truth), the overwhelming reason for these women being targeted is their vulnerability. Sex workers in most countries across the world are extremely vulnerable. Most often, their work is criminalised and they are at high risk of violence from their customers, and sometimes from law enforcement too. It is this vulnerability that attracts American serial killers to these victims. This will also be true in other countries where the large majority of citizens are not exceptionally fragile or easy targets, but it is not true in South Africa.

If predators seek out easy targets – the proverbial wounded antelopes – the vast majority of the South African herd is incapacitated in some way. Poverty, unemployment, lack of education and an overall pervading sense of desperation for survival under enormous strain result in a huge portion of our population being overwhelmingly vulnerable. In South Africa, and many other countries with similar socioeconomic backdrops, serial murderers do not have to go very far to find the wounded antelope, and they certainly don't need to target sex workers specifically. Very simply, their possible victim pool is far larger.

While South African sex workers certainly remain at risk of violence, they are not the chosen victim of local serial murderers. A study that appeared in the 2015 issue of *Journal of Investigative Psychology and Offender Profiling* focused on 54 solved murder series in South Africa between 1936 and 2007 and it showed that just eight per cent of those victims were sex workers.

Of course, as luck would have it, two of the serial murderers in this book did target sex workers. Michael, who appears later, is one; Kyle is the other.

Kyle's first recorded victim was discovered by a passerby one summer morning in December 1992. The woman, Mary Marais, who was a known sex worker in the area, had been stabbed to death. Mary was naked from the waist down and lying on her back on the stairs of a municipal building. The autopsy would show severe lacerations to her vagina, which may have been indicative of rape with a foreign object.

Rape with a foreign object in serial murder is an important part of the modus operandi, as it can be used to link murders to one another. Interestingly, many of the sex-worker murder series in South Africa have involved foreign-body insertion of some kind. This is despite the fact that prostitutes being targeted by serial murderers, and foreign-body insertion, are both rare on their own. Most simply, foreign-body insertion could be seen as a way to inflict intimate, sadistic violence. The psychology behind foreign-body insertion during a rape could involve the offender either physically not being able to perform the rape himself (the feelings of inadequacy around this might well add to the level of violence in the act) or the insertion forming part of the offender's fantasy around the sexually motivated murder.

Murders of sex workers are either not well investigated or are difficult to solve simply because of the nature of stranger murders. Mary's murder was no different, and it would remain unsolved for eight years.

Just one month after Mary was murdered, though, yet another sex worker lost her life in the same area. On the fateful night, three sex workers hanging out at a local bar, which was usually a good place to pick up customers, left with a man who said he intended to use the services of at least one of the women.

The two women who survived the night would later report to police that the man had chosen their friend, Amber Vermaak. He and Amber had left the other two on the side of the road, driving further on down the road to complete their transaction. The man had said that he would come back for the women when he and Amber were finished, and give them a lift back into town. About half an hour later, though, the women had seen the man driving back down the road alone in the vehicle. There was also a dent in the car that hadn't been there when he'd left.

Concerned about Amber, the women started walking up the road looking for her. They found her, deceased, under some bushes. She had a head injury – a skull fracture, which a pathologist would later determine had been caused by a blow from a rock. While this had been her cause of death, she had clearly endured significant horrors prior to passing away. When Amber's friends found her, a wine bottle had been inserted into her vagina. The women were so horrified at the discovery, and their mistrust of the police ran so deep, that they fled the scene and did not notify the authorities. Before leaving, though, the women, perhaps wanting to reclaim some of Amber's dignity, removed the bottle from her vagina and flung it into the bushes.

Amber's body would be discovered for a second time later that night by a homeless man who did call the police. When the police arrived, they discovered a stick driven into Amber's private parts. It was only after Amber's two friends were located and the full picture could be put together that it became clear that in the period between Amber's friends leaving her body and the homeless man finding her, the killer had returned to the scene. Clearly unhappy at his handiwork having been disturbed, he had sought to repeat the indignity with another object.

Although Amber's friends gave the police a description of the offender and his vehicle, he was not traced at the time, and the sex-worker series that had started up suddenly stopped. The delay would be explained later, after the offender was arrested, but it would be a full seven years before another body was found.

The third known victim in this series was not a sex worker, but the offender's later explanation of the circumstances of her death would reveal her to be vulnerable in a different sense, as a single mother who needed shelter with her young son. When her body was found in 1996 in a green bin liner behind a building, her identity was unknown. The offender would later claim that her first name was Sydney, but no further identification was ever made. Her murder also remained unsolved – and also not linked to the two murdered sex workers seven years before either.

It's not uncommon for serial killers to be caught in ways completely unconnected to their initial series. Some get pulled over for speeding; others trip themselves up by sending messages to the police or journalists or calling in to news stations. For this offender it would, unfortunately, be another murder, but one completely different from his previous crimes.

In mid-December 2000, police were called to a boarding house where residents had discovered the body of one of their housemates in a large dustbin in the street outside. The victim, Simon Harris, was a young man who had been staying at the house for a few months. He had been strangled to death. On searching his room, the police found traces of blood and also noted that the mattress had been removed; it would later be found cut into pieces in the same dustbin in which Simon's body had been found.

Residents reported that Simon had last been seen with another housemate, Kyle Kennedy. The two men had been drinking together the previous night, and no one had seen either man since, until they'd discovered Simon's body.

Kennedy was arrested four days later, walking the streets, still dressed in a blood-splattered shirt.

During questioning, Kennedy admitted to Simon's murder, although he claimed it was self-defence in that the man had attacked him with a shifting spanner. Detectives found this difficult to believe, considering Simon had been strangled to death, which is not a very common method of defence against an implement attack.

Kennedy went on to admit to the murder of a woman he identified only as Sydney, as well as Amber Vermaak and Mary Marais. He also claimed that he had killed another sex worker before he had killed Sydney, but police could never trace the case he referred to. It emerged that the long pause in his murders was due to his having been imprisoned for an attempted murder that had occurred during a housebreaking.

He pleaded guilty and was handed down four life sentences.

Kyle's killer story

I am meeting the man who arrested Kyle Kennedy. He's older than the other detectives and dressed neatly in a sleeveless pullover. His politeness and his precision remind me of my high-school choir master.

We spread the case papers over his desk, and lean over them as we discuss Kyle's crimes. I crush his lunchtime sandwich with my elbow, and he waves off my embarrassed apologies, intent on helping. The detective comments that Kyle comes across as cultured, and changes his language from English to Afrikaans and vice versa, as well as his opinions, to try to get you on his side.

Kyle is a slim, athletically built, white man of medium height, dressed in short-sleeved dark-green prison fatigues. He has black hair and beard, and gaps between his chipped teeth. 'I'm not a serial killer,' he says, before I've even turned on the tape recorder, and before the consent forms are signed. Speaking to him is an onslaught. He speaks a *lot*. We talk through five-and-a-half hours of tape that day, and he keeps talking even when the recorder is off while I change tapes. And, as the detective predicted, he matches his language to mine: when I speak English, he does; when I change to Afrikaans, so does he.

It is important to Kyle that he is seen in a positive light. He avoids negative events and facts. He denies or explains away emotions that could be perceived as antisocial. This makes it hard to keep the thread of his story: as soon as I try, Kyle changes the topic and the narrative zips away to another time and place. These switchback changes in direction, almost mid-sentence, happen especially when we're discussing anything negative about him.

He sprinkles his narrative with references to his virtues or his attractiveness. That's not to suggest he is without positive qualities but, in the context, there's something darkly comical about their incongruous grandiosity; it's like a scene out of a cringe-comedy.

I struggle to keep pace with the interview in the flurry of switches of topic, deflections and self-praise. Audibly paddling hard, my initial comments are mostly limited to laughing and saying, 'Oh, ja.'

Kyle has a long scar from his ear to the edge of his lip, grooved white through the stubble on his face. 'I was cut here, on the face, not long ago,' he says, clearly irritated, and mentions a date five months previously, then adds, 'An inner calmness was inside me. No one could understand, but the calmness and joy the Lord gives is unbelievable.'

Kyle then explains that while working in the kitchen, a fellow prisoner had spent days provoking him, mocking him. The crisis came after three days when he 'went for me': his opponent's glance at an urn of boiling water made Kyle think he was planning to throw it at him. Kyle wasn't worried about his being struck – 'I am very quick' – but more that the people behind him might be burnt. 'So I hit him in the head. I didn't want to fight, but it was necessary.' As his opponent dropped, the other people were 'very stupid, and grabbed me instead of him', and that was when the man leapt up and slashed Kyle with a knife.

(I later hear another version of the same fight story, from another prisoner, who says the fight happened in a cell, not in the kitchen; there was no boiling water, no heroic defence of others. 'Kyle almost killed him,' this man says.)

I suspect Kyle dislikes the piratical appearance the healing knife wound gives him: 'I can't get used to it. That's why I am growing a beard, even though I don't like a beard … I'm upset about it, but the Lord wants me in different ways.'

Later, he expands on this, in a discussion about the 'horrible temper' he had as a child: 'my brother was a bully. I never fought back but sometimes violence is necessary,' he says.

> BH: In what situations?
> KK: Like this guy who cut me in the face.

I am not sure, at the end of the interview, that I know Kyle any better. My attempts at probing to find chinks in the armour of words does not seem to yield much. I can hear my own ironic exasperation in the tape when, just before I turn it off, I mumble, 'Ladies and gentlemen, Elvis has left the building.'

Later Kyle posts me drawings he made: Mickey Mouse, Donald Duck, hearts and flowers. They tell me nothing about the man, and a lot about the performance. This swirling performance, I later realise, is part of the fog.

Kyle's story tips you straight into the criminal underworld of the coastal city in which he operated. His associates all seem to be criminals, drug addicts, people scratching a survival in the seedy underbelly of everyday life, gangsters out to prey on those around them: women, children, vulnerable men in desperate need of protection from the cruel world.

Everyone in Kyle's world is linked together by a Byzantine network of debts owed, grudges and secret plots set to entrap or trip him up. Many of the incidents Kyle tells me about are propelled by this: owing someone money, a sudden argument coming out of nowhere, always with an opaque back story.

This network is overseen by the first character Kyle talks about: Dr Adam Mohammed. Kyle compares Mohammed with the arch-villain in the TV soap opera *Days of Our Lives*. Like this fictional antagonist, Mohammed holds all the threads in a web of criminal enterprise; he is almost supernaturally wealthy, influential and able to manipulate events.

> I worked for Mohammed as a driver, bodyguard, chauffeur, but actually I was working against him, for the government. That is why I am sitting here today, because I know too much. My life is in danger outside. But I would rather be outside in danger than in this place.

Kyle reports having founded his own company, Minotaur Security Services, providing debt collectors and nightclub bouncers. He mentions all the well-known detectives he apparently worked for and is friends with. He proudly displays his ID book, stuffed with business cards from police officers and other people involved in the fight against crime.

He refers often to his military service, and the fact he was trained to fight bare-handed. 'I'm an ex-private investigator, an ex-military policeman, a security specialist.' In the murky and ever-shifting criminal milieu within which he works, these various roles do not sound entirely implausible. 'I can handle it,' he says, talking about violent situations he encountered as a bouncer.

Many of the situations he tells me about imply his role was to provide 'muscle', wherever and whenever it was needed. He takes pains to clarify, however, that he is soft-hearted, dislikes violence, is known to be affectionate, and is 'a man of great discipline'.

The picture Kyle initially paints of himself is one of a man of action, doing his best to protect people in an unkind universe: a foil to the dark, corrupting power of Dr Mohammed. 'I'm a person that, if I can help a person, I will help them.' He describes helping people clean their flats, volunteering to clear their gardens, taking their dogs for a walk or protecting their children. At various points he warns people about Dr Mohammed's threats to their life, houses people for their protection, gives money to the poor and finds accommodation for the vulnerable. People knew him, he says, as a 'nice person, and a bodyguard to lots of people'. These episodes of his helping others are some of the most crucial in his narrative.

Quite often, though, this erstwhile altruism comes at a cost to Kyle.

> The problem with me is that I get so fond of people, I don't want to leave them, I take them as a family. I'm a person who would give his life for his friends. [The person later] lets me down. That is one thing I can't handle: disappointment. I trust people [so] that is very hard for me to handle. The problem is I get people who disappoint me so badly, I am scared to make friends again.

As the detective who arrested Kyle had predicted, he does not want to talk about his family. When we discuss them, his body language changes. His usually open posture closes up, his arms cross.

His narration of his family history is confusing and hard to follow. 'My parents were Nazis,' he says. 'I was raised a racist.' Then he describes their firm religious convictions, and the rift between his mother's and father's families due to differing Christian beliefs. 'Everything is drawn back to religion,' my interview notes record: 'brute-force religious beliefs.'

His mother was the main caregiver, loving and artistic, possessive and jealous. He describes his father as anger-filled, and mostly indifferent to his children. He would give 'proper hidings. He wasn't the sort of person to talk to you, he would just give a hiding and be finished with you.'

Kyle was the second-youngest of seven children, and the youngest boy. His first sexual experience was when his second-eldest brother forced the 12-year-old Kyle to have sex with his sister. His two eldest brothers are mentioned often as violent bullies.

In the statement he made when arrested, confessing to the murders for which he was imprisoned, he painted a vivid picture of his youth: fighting with teachers, getting involved with gangs, drinking turpentine and sniffing petrol, being forced to live in a small caravan outside his parents' house. 'I was a little gangster,' he chuckled.

When he was 14, Kyle was taken to a place of safety by welfare.

BH: What were the reasons for the welfare to take you?
KK: My parents were Nazis and all those things. I used
      to run away from school. They classified me as
      'uncontrollable' at school. Because I was always first
      against the leaders. It was always one against a lot.

Kyle repeats this pattern throughout his life: fighting relentlessly against others whom he believes to have wronged him, a victim of the power they share by ganging up on him. He sees other people as frequently unjust and wrong-minded, ganging up on him as an innocent.

Kyle, missing his mother, soon ran away.

Those people at the welfare looked down on us as criminals.
They were bullies, untrustworthy. The welfare are meant to
help you with problems, but they just take you to a place of
safety and forget about you. You're not their problem.

'I was too much for various schools,' says Kyle, who was eventually sent away to a reformatory ('worse than prison') on the other side of the country. He describes the effort they would put into making the school neat when visited by an important person. 'They'll give us nice food just for that day,' he recalls, then, when the visitors left, everything would go back to normal. Linking the school to the state, he dismisses them all: 'the whole government is corrupt in my eyes.'

His confession statement contained a lengthy section describing his battle with 'gangs' in that school. Nose broken and ear damaged from a battle with them, he escaped from hospital and was again attacked by the combined manpower of two school hostels. 'The school took the gangs' side,' he said. 'They would rather take the leaders' advice over me, because I am one against many.'

In a segue typical of his life story, he continues that he dislikes macho gang members, and says that he refuses to show respect to the prison gangs.

There are three main gangs in South African prisons: the 26s, the 27s and the 28s. The prison gangs are a hundred years old, predating the formation of the South African prison service. They operate in all prisons in the country. Their elaborate structures, ranks and disciplinary codes mimic the traditional Zulu army, the militaristic structures of the South African apartheid system, and the prison administration itself. Each gang has its traditions, secret codes and language, and roles in prison.

> To me [a gang member is] nothing. And that's what they can't handle. I know what I'm capable of. I'm a good fighter and everything but I'll always show I'm a much better person.

Kyle left school for good halfway through Standard 9 (today's Grade 11): 'I wanted to make matric, but because of the unright-eousness, I forced myself out of school and into the army.' The army seemed a better fit for him.

> When I was in the army I could really take revenge because I was a military policeman. Now all those people who attacked me, I could get them all back. But I am not like that, to take revenge, any more, because the Lord said he's the one to avenge, and I take it very seriously.

During his time in the army, he reports being stabbed in the heart while carrying out his duties as a military policeman, seeing a friend killed in combat in Namibia, and being beaten almost to death by 'the enemy'. Despite this, he enjoyed the army and wanted to stay.

> BH: Why did you leave?
> KK: When I had a fight in the army, I got hit with a big rock. They took this guy's side instead of my side, and I couldn't take it. I just gave it up. I was disappointed because I liked the army.

11

Kyle doesn't describe precisely why he returned to his home town, and he doesn't present a clear chronology of events. His work record appears to have been erratic. There was employment he is quick to mention – an assistant manager for an industrial company, for example, or founding Minotaur Security Services and a second company, Professional Bouncers, where he would train ex-army personnel to work in clubs; his role as a club bouncer seemed to be one he enjoyed.

There was employment with Dr Mohammed and others who needed someone who, as Kyle framed it, would be able to keep order; this was more stressful as he was 'secretly working against' his employer with undercover police officers. The stress led him to drink heavily. Kyle's drinking became associated with his offences.

Then there was employment that he mentioned almost accidentally, and quickly moved the conversation away from, such as being a male prostitute for both men and women. 'Very good pay, no tax,' he laughs, although he is quick to confirm he did the former only when very poor, and stopped the latter as it was 'against God'.

He reports being very popular with women, having four serious relationships over this time and numerous girlfriends. He says he was deeply committed to his serious girlfriends (usually calling them 'fiancées') and was an excellent, considerate lover and partner; he studied magazines, he said, to find ways to better please women. Unfortunately, each relationship ended in betrayal and disappointment, and although the precise circumstances behind breakups are unclear, Kyle concludes that women are 'untrustworthy'.

Through the late 1980s and into the 1990s, Kyle's list of criminal convictions grew. These brushes with the law are presented as sudden, unexpected potholes in his life. His explanations are unclear, but follow a pattern: Kyle is trying his best to be a good person, then is suddenly tripped up by unlucky circumstances, the actions of other people, or other opaque external influences.

He was imprisoned for theft and fraud while an assistant manager, and he explains that this happened as the company was not paying him for commissions and expenses he was due. 'I work my ass off,' he says. He implies that he returned any money he took without permission but 'they charged me, with theft and fraud'.

He describes a charge for attempted murder when he stepped in to defend a woman who was being attacked by her partner: 'This guy hit this woman's jaw off. Now, this man is a bit big for me but I defended myself, and I gave him a clout.' In court, the state lawyer he was assigned turned all the blame for the event on Kyle and his fiancée, and he got four years, although, Kyle insists, it was 'that guy fighting with his wife'.

He laughs and says that he was arrested again on the same street, for a near identical case.

KK: There is a fluke on that street.
BH: What happened [that] time?
KK: Also a man who was fighting with a woman. I can't
     stand seeing a man hitting a woman. I am just that way.
     Maybe it's because of seeing my dad hitting my mom.

In a third incident, Kyle says that he had lost his house (seemingly due to Dr Mohammed) and was forced to move into a single room with his fiancée, on condition that he became the owner's assistant, 'sorting it out' if there was a problem with drink or drugs. One evening, Kyle had a domestic disagreement with his fiancée. It's a confusing muddle of late-night socialisation, implied infidelity, not being able to resolve disagreements due to crowded living conditions: 'I didn't know what happened; I was very upset,' concludes Kyle.

By apparent unlucky coincidence, a man and his wife then started fighting in the same block of flats, and Kyle had to go and investigate, otherwise he would lose his accommodation. A brawl ensued. Kyle was stabbed, his fiancée stabbed the man who stabbed him, and a pot was smashed on Kyle's head. 'The police found me and this other guy having a fight and they put us both in the bakkie.' The fight seemed to have continued in the police van.

Kyle was shocked to find himself blamed for the events of that night.

The whole case was such a corruption. If I really planned
to kill a guy, I would have killed him, finished, and leave no

evidence behind. The whole thing was so corrupt. There were no witnesses in court. I don't know what happened there.

He was even more shocked when, during one of his assault trials, an ex-fiancée laid a charge of rape against him. He says it was her revenge on him for hitting her after she abused her baby. He claims she threw her baby across the room, and he 'smacked her with a backhand, and said, "Never do that again; a child is a gift from God."' He says this annoyed her and 'because she is a scorpion, she waited three to four months to take revenge in court. I couldn't talk, I was crying, I was upset.'

By this stage he was already under suspicion of the murder of Amber. He describes feeling defeated by the unfairness of the system and the accusations against him, accepting the four life sentences he was handed down. In his account, at the time all this was happening, he was working undercover to help save Dr Mohammed's victims, and in one case he head-butted Mohammed 'because he treated people so badly'.

Kyle's style of storytelling makes it hard to link his descriptions to crimes listed in his record. What is clear is that he was convicted for many more crimes than he disclosed to me when I asked. In the 13 years before his arrest for the murders, he was convicted of assault twice, of theft on four separate occasions (with numerous counts in each charge), of fraud twice (again on multiple counts), of drunk driving and of damaging property (twice); he had convictions for rape with assault, house breaking with intention to murder, attempted murder, and assault with the intention to cause grievous boldly harm. It is difficult to reconcile these hard judicial facts with Kyle's depiction of himself as a man just trying to do his job, and treat people fairly, laid low by corruption and bad luck.

The simplest explanation would be that he is lying. Kyle knows the true facts of what he did and wilfully conceals them to escape blame. The confused and fragmented nature of his inner story hinders deeper understanding, however, and I start to wonder whether Kyle is actually unable to bring together all the facts of his life, draw the links between them, and so get deeper insight into what he is like. For example, Kyle is aware he has (or had) a terrible temper.

> KK: I can get very angry but I changed now. I get
>   aggressive but I get over it quickly.
> BH: What was it like before?
> KK: Say I get cross with you, I will beat the life out of you.

He mentions several events when he has stepped in to defend people and then somehow got the blame. Yet he doesn't link the two, perhaps because this would mean accepting the blame for the number of assaults of which he has been convicted. Instead, he implies his reputation for anger is a virtue in prison.

> I have a temper. A lot of people respect me because I'm straightforward. Some people are getting scared about it because they're not used to the straightforwardness. That's the way I am. I can't change it.

In similar vein, Kyle's story is peppered with anecdotes of his helping people. He often repeats his desire to help and protect others. While it's hard to tell whether this is signalling imagined virtue or a genuine desire to help others, what is clear is that many of his attempts end with Kyle coming into violent conflict with the person he is trying to help. Yet rather than draw the link between attempted helpfulness and poor outcomes, Kyle persists.

If we believe his account, that is exactly what led to the murder of Simon Harris. When Kyle was brought before a magistrate in the late 1990s, he had just been arrested on suspicion of murdering Simon. Still bloodied from the final struggle, he says he wanted to confess in order to be put under psychological observation to find out 'what's wrong with me' and get the 'necessary operations' for the injuries to his mouth and shoulders.

His 27-page confession is a rambling document, and a new set of plot lines and characters. They are all along similar themes: his being under the influence of other people and shadowy organisations; his religious beliefs and commitment; people ganging up on him. He confessed to five murders, eventually being convicted of four: those of Simon Harris, Sydney, Amber Vermaak and Mary Marais. (His alleged fifth victim was never found.)

He pleaded guilty initially. However, when I speak to him just over two years later, his story of what had happened has been rewritten. Kyle employs tactics used by defence lawyers, who challenge the police's version of events, picking at crucial details and processes, casting doubt on the motivations of the witnesses and pointing out mitigations for guilt. Defence lawyers do this to prevent miscarriages of justice, making sure the justice system does what it has been designed to do, without fear or favour.

Kyle's motives are altogether less noble, though. He never quite claims that he is innocent. He certainly implies, though, that he cannot possibly be guilty. 'I was positive I was going to walk out the case,' he insists, but he goes on to lament that in the cases of Simon and Sydney, Mohammed's influence made sure the charges against him stuck. 'He cleared it so beautifully.'

The detective's assessment of the murder of Simon Harris was not charitable to Kyle. Simon was an alcoholic and terminally ill. After a drinking session, he and Kyle got into an argument about an unpaid debt. Kyle snuck into Simon's room, attacked him with a spanner, strangled him and put his body into a dustbin, with his cut-up mattress stuffed on top.

Kyle's account differs. Simon, in Kyle's story, was an alcoholic mess who spent his days squatting on a dirty mattress in the middle of the floor: 'There was something psychologically wrong with him.' That night, Simon was sitting on his mattress, narrates Kyle, and he agreed to help Simon, to 'prepare him nicely', and to take him to the bar, shaved, ready for a night out.

> Everything was prepared, and when I tapped this guy on the shoulder, he hit me with a shifting spanner. It all happened very fast. I hit him once or twice. I hit him, and I kicked him on the Adam's apple. I put him in the bin, and said, 'Sorry, Simon, you forced me.'

He shows me the scars on his inner lip, the two teeth he lost, and says he still has damage to his left ear.

'In the beginning, I thought I was responsible for his death but later on,' Kyle continues, as the story of the night's events were retold in court, 'I thought, Hey, no, there's a mistake somewhere.'

Kyle remembers leaving Simon on the stoep, knowing some friends would shortly be at the flat to fetch Simon to go out clubbing. 'Then I hit a blank or whatever and woke up at hospital.'

By the time of our interview, Kyle has reflected more deeply on the event. With the benefit of this reflection, he re-narrates the offence. He lists numerous provocations from Simon. He suggests that Simon was 'running away from somebody, I don't know who'. He says witnesses were scared to tell the truth, or bribed with drugs, or 'that Mohammed must have paid a lot of people to lie'. He points out discrepancies he spotted in the case files ('He fell back on the coffee table, but the photo shows that the coffee table is standing in an upright position').

In the case of the woman, Sydney, Kyle says, 'Mohammed told me to go kill those people who lived in the place, get rid of them, in my own way; he doesn't [want to] know how.' 'Those people' were Sydney, her young son and a man.

Sydney, says Kyle, 'showered and everything and had a decent job. I never knew she had a second job as a prostitute.' (We only have Kyle's word for this.) He says that he told Sydney that she and her son could stay in a flat behind where he was staying. Sydney, who Kyle describes as not his 'kind of woman', was 'forced' to sleep in his bed with him, presumably for protection.

The man with her, 'who was not a healthy person and who didn't like to bath', was asked by Kyle to leave. An acquaintance of his would tell detectives this was typical of Kyle, who would force his attention on women.

Describing the events that ended in Sydney's death, Kyle says

We had an argument. When I told her to stand, she refused. I wanted to pull her out the chair to make her go. Now, the chair was very antique – Mohammed likes to buy old antique things, that's where he makes his extra money. I don't know what she klapped [drank] but she went limp in my hands. I think she passed out from alcohol.

In his confession, he said he thought he had snapped her neck. Again, 'things happened fast.'

He then goes on to demonstrate all the reasons why he should not have been found guilty of the murder. He says he had left Sydney safely in the back room. He mentions crowds of people out causing trouble that night; he says that, at that time, he was engaged in a struggle with local gangsters. 'The evidence shows she was dead from a knife stab, so I don't know what happened.' Witnesses were mentally ill. He says that he had put a dead dog in the green bag Sydney was found in, tied it with a shoelace (in his confession he specified the bag had been tied with white nylon string) and given it to 'some crazy guy' with satanic markings on his face. He can't understand how Sydney ended up in the bag, tied with a nylon string.

His retellings of the other murders were similar. Amber Vermaak, found with her head smashed in and objects inserted in her vagina, had certainly not been murdered by him.

BH: How did Amber die?
KK: I'm not sure. So many things [were] said in court. I'm not sure. I think the people who were witnesses in the case were themselves involved.

He then talks through all the discrepancies he noted in the case, picking through things he says don't make sense. Why did the man who killed Amber not come back and kill the other two? Why would he use his car to pick up prostitutes when he could as easily have done it in a bar or pub? How could the other two women have walked all that way back and found Amber's body in the dark? The bottle inserted in the victim was variously described as 750 ml and 1 litre – maybe it had been swapped? If they had removed the bottle, who then put in the stick, and with such great force that it punctured an intestine? They said the victim was killed in one place and moved to another: 'Now, that doesn't make sense to me.'

BH: What do you think happened?
KK: I don't know. The whole court case doesn't make sense to me.

Kyle gives a number of scenarios for what happened to Amber: a fight with other prostitutes? A boyfriend? He keeps repeating, 'I don't know,' pausing, thinking out loud and describing problems. Faced with his flurry of questions, it is easy to get confused in all the cross-checking. It's easy to forget all the witnesses, circumstances and forensic evidence that led to his convictions.

Finally, what about Mary Marais, the sex worker who was found partly undressed at the top of a concrete stairwell in the town centre? She had been stabbed to death. There was also evidence of violent rape.

In his confession, Kyle said he had killed her under the influence of an extreme right-wing sect to which his then-girlfriend belonged. He said he stabbed her with a knife provided especially. Yet, in our interview, a different tale is told. He was approached by a woman on the street who pulled a knife on him, he says, and was either going to rob him or kill him, but he took the knife from her, stabbed her in the arm 'or something', dropped the knife and ran away.

> These things happen these days: a prostitute will lure you and rob you. Now, this woman they found on the steps, she wasn't stabbed with a knife alone.

He points out that she was stabbed a number of times, with different knives, and concludes that 'there is something not right with this case either'.

As with Sydney and Simon, Kyle gives himself motive, places himself at the scene in the precise scenario, then finds discrepancies to help explain why it could not, in fact, be his fault. He concludes that, in addition to Mohammed's bribery, the lawyers and judiciary manipulated him in court. He was enraged when the prosecutor called him 'a danger to society', and white-faced with anger when he was convicted.

> KK: [The press] called me a serial killer, and I am not. I'm very upset about it.
> BH: How would you describe yourself, as a reply to the newspapers?

> KK: I am a protector of people. I like to protect people.
> I'm very helpful. I'm a lovable person. Whenever I am
> outside, or even sat in prison, when there is trouble I
> will try to stop it. That's not what the court sees. They
> think I'm one crazy maniac.

Kyle's story is hard to follow. He's simultaneously working for and against Dr Mohammed, a gangster overlord of seemingly limitless malice, cunning and money, with the ability to influence anyone, anywhere. In this tale, Kyle is an ex-soldier and military policeman who does his best to help everyone around him, trying to do the right thing in a corrupt world. This narrative explains much of what happened and, when it doesn't, then it was corrupt, sly or mentally ill people working to throw Kyle off his path in life.

Kyle is not psychotic, that is, he has not so lost touch with reality that he has no idea what is real and what isn't. Yes, there is always the simple explanation that he is making things up in the hope that a young and gullible researcher will believe him. But this simple explanation misses an essential question: why? Why would Kyle make things up that he knows to be untrue? He is in prison. I have been clear that the interview results will not make any difference to any appeal or retrial.

Perhaps maintaining his story helps him maintain his sense of self. Telling me that he is essentially a good person, misled and misunderstood, helps him believe that himself. He keeps himself blind to his story to avoid having to deal with the impact this would have on him. This also helps him avoid guilt over his crimes. According to the detective who arrested him, 'He genuinely believes that he is innocent.'

This glib acceptance of the easiest and most familiar story is understandable. This avoidance has consequences, though. By avoiding listening to the stories we tell ourselves, we are in danger from our secret selves.

I can understand why Kyle might tell this story to himself when I contrast his confused but heroic epic with a different version of his story told using the same events: Kyle is a lifelong criminal, constantly in and out of prison, struggling with drink, childhood trauma and his own violent temper. No wonder he'd want to reduce the dissonance.

Kyle sometimes quivers on the edge of making the link between elements of his life, such as his temper and the murders, but then he diverts attention, skipping to another part of the narrative or recalling another of his virtues. And when he can't explain away any alleged ill behaviour, then the deeper fog descends and 'I don't know what happened there'.

In many ways, Kyle's story recalls how life really can often feel: messy and chaotic. Things happen suddenly, out of the blue, and without clear reasons. Events have unknown causes and unpredictable effects, and there is little chance to reflect. The meaning behind each of Kyle's anecdotes is unclear, and in the absence of a story's ability to give structure and meaning, Kyle simply reacts. Without a story to make sense of his life, he appears to make the same mistakes over and over again. Fragments of contradictory stories drive contradictory behaviours.

Kyle's habits of deflecting the conversation, switching between topics, continually reassuring himself that he is really a good person, may be the result of his own volatile inner world. However, they do something else to his narrative: they keep his story foggy. The warm blanket of fog is comfortable: wrapped in it, he never has to deal with the clash between who he believes himself to be and who he actually is.

There is another factor, though, that makes the fog so powerful. The fog, you see, is not just something passive. It doesn't just cloak your story and make it hard to see what is really happening. It has a darker active layer. This active layer continually gnaws away at any narrative that threatens the fog. It doesn't need to create its own, better story. It's simply enough that any story that is becoming strong enough to threaten the fog is nibbled to pieces by a thousand small doubts and questions.

You see this in action when Kyle describes the murders for which he was convicted: Mary Marais being killed as part of an extremist ritual collapsed under the lack of evidence in court, so Kyle created a fresh narrative, one where there was some sort of attempted robbery. This doesn't explain Mary's being found undressed and violently raped, but it doesn't need to; it's just enough to cast doubt. It doesn't need to persuade a court, either; it just needs to convince Kyle himself. If the fog succeeds in this job, then Kyle will never need to be confronted with the consequences of his actions. He never needs to go through the grinding effort required to change himself. Best of all, he will never be in the wrong. Ever.

In terms of narrative psychology, the fog isn't just an inability to make the events of your life into a coherent story. It goes deeper. It is an inability to see the narratives you are living out in your life; it's as if your story is hidden by a fog, drifting in and out of focus. The individual pieces don't fit together. The words don't match the actions. The overall meaning is lost. The story ambushes you suddenly, having led you into a plot twist you didn't see coming. This fog means that even to the person living the story, the story is not immediately obvious.

This is the first killer story: the fog. By denying everything, you stifle your narrative.

2 Jacques: Isolation

The crimes

The young man was home alone, and bored. He sat on his parents'
couch, calculating how much time he had before they returned. He
decided he had enough time to satiate this profound boredom, at
least temporarily.

There was only one way to do it. He'd learnt that.

It had started with petty thefts from his mother's handbag –
pocketing a few notes from her purse while she pottered in the
kitchen. The rush was exhilarating, and he'd briefly wondered if this
was what it was like to feel things. The surge had become addictive,
and he'd soon found he needed to do more and more to achieve
the same result. That was how he'd found his way into Thomasina
Selepeng's room that day.

Thomasina was asleep in her room in the back of the property
when her assailant entered. She awoke on hearing the door opening
and started to scream. To stop her from resisting, he punched her in
the stomach, but the terrified woman continued to fight back.

The cause of Thomasina's death would be recorded by the
police as strangulation. An autopsy examination would later be
unable to determine whether she had been raped, as, by the time
she was discovered, her body had sustained burns from the fire her
killer had started in her room.

For almost three years, Thomasina Selepeng's murder remained unsolved.

Two years after he had killed her, her murderer felt the need to experience that ultimate rush again, and the deadly cycle restarted.

Wrapped in the warm comfort of her bed, 37-year-old Sylvia Claassen didn't stir as the stranger entered her flat. The man did not stumble about in the dark: he'd been there before. The woman had been unaware of his presence on that occasion too. That day, the man had picked up the keys to her car and taken it for a joyride. The thrill he'd experienced from this brazen act was increased by the speed at which he drove – and the knowledge that the woman's flat was right next door to his workplace.

Anyone could have seen him that night, but no one had, and he'd simply returned the vehicle to its parking spot and tossed the key back through an open window – there was always a window open in the woman's flat.

On this evening, though, as the man entered the flat for the second time, things were different. Although he would later say that he hadn't planned to harm anyone, he crept into her bedroom as she slept and started to remove his clothing. The woman stirred, then opened her eyes to find him standing naked beside her bed. As the horrifying reality of what was happening began to dawn, the blanket of sleep was ripped away: she understood that every woman's nightmare was about to be visited on her. What she did not know was that the man had already killed one woman.

In response to her demand to know what he wanted, he produced a 9 mm pistol – an unspoken threat to comply, or else. She attempted to placate the intruder by telling him that he didn't look like a violent person. Unfortunately, this seemed to infuriate the man and a struggle ensued. He raped her, and when he was finished, he tossed the duvet over her. Before leaving, he ripped the landline telephone out of the wall.

This was the start of a pattern: the perpetrator recce'd homes beforehand and often entered them for the purposes of theft, before returning to take what he really wanted.

Sixty-two-year-old Jane Ferreira lived in a flat close to the other crime scenes. The assailant had entered her home during a day while she was sitting in her lounge. She had been unaware of his presence. He had rifled through her handbag and stolen R20.

That night, between midnight and 2 am, he returned. The lights were off in Jane's flat, and the sound of her level breathing filled the air as he tiptoed into the bedroom. She woke up and screamed at him. He clubbed her with the pistol and she stopped screaming. He pulled off the duvet, removed her clothes, raped her, and fled the scene.

After this rape, police recognised that there was a serial rapist in the area and an operation was set up to catch him. Investigators could have no idea, however, how close the man they were looking for actually was.

The next home that was struck had been under surveillance by the offender for some time. He'd broken into the house four or five times before his final – and deadly – entry, and he knew the layout quite well. Despite this knowledge, the house was a risky hit. The residence was a shared house of sorts, and both men and women lived there. While the assailant had identified a specific woman he wanted to rape, when he broke in on the night in question, he ended up in the bedroom of a different woman.

Twenty-seven-year-old Rebecca Strydom woke up to light flooding her room as a strange man flicked on the switch. She struggled against the intruder, but he struck her and then raped her at gunpoint. Then, while still lying on top of her, he raised the weapon to her head and pulled the trigger.

Rebecca was found lying in bed, with her duvet pulled up to her chin. Her left hand showed what appeared to be a defensive wound: she may have lifted it up to her head to try to shield herself from the shot and the bullet had grazed her hand.

Two weeks later, the assailant struck again, breaking into another apartment he'd been watching for some time. His reconnaissance had told him that two women lived in the home, and that one window was always left open. He made entry under cover of darkness and found both bedroom doors partially open. While he stood in the darkened home preparing to choose one of the doors, one of the occupants woke, needing to use the toilet.

As she opened her bedroom door, 27-year-old Belinda Wiley found herself face to face with a strange man. She screamed, and he hit her on the head with the butt of his gun. She collapsed. He dragged her to her bed, undressed her and raped her. Her naked body was found in the bathtub by her flatmate the following morning.

Police picked up a stubbed-out cigarette near the door of the bathroom, which would later be attributed to the assailant. They also found, and took moulds of, footprints at the scene.

All the crimes had, up to that point, been committed in close proximity to the police barracks and investigators began to suspect that their killer lived there. As much as they didn't want to believe it, they had to consider that the serial rapist and murderer they sought was one of their own.

They had recovered fingerprints from several of the crime scenes and so a fingerprinting exercise was arranged, with all officers living at the hostel instructed to attend. The exercise did not provide any definitive results – but the offender did seem to be concerned that the police may be closing in, as he did not commit any further crimes for the following four months.

When the series started up again, the offender had changed his geographical area of operation.

Seventy-four-year-old Margaret Welwyn lived alone in her flat and was therefore a perfect target for a criminal of this nature. The man got into her home by squeezing through an open window. In the bedroom, he flipped the light on. Margaret did not stir.

After rummaging through her handbag and taking some cash, he noticed a torch on a nearby table. Picking it up, he switched it on and the main light off. He approached the still-sleeping Margaret with the torch and his pistol. She woke up as soon as he touched her and immediately began to struggle, grabbing at his hands. As the pair fought, the man fired a single shot into Margaret's face. The bullet hit her in the mouth, knocking out some of her teeth.

This victim was not raped.

Two months later, a few items were stolen from a home in the area.

Two weeks after this theft, 16-year-old Judith Schoeman was home alone, save for a gardener working in the front yard, when, to her horror, she was confronted by a strange man. She screamed and tried to run away but he grabbed her and dragged her to a bedroom. He closed the door and pulled her shirt off.

Judith told the man that there was money in her mother's bedroom and that he could have it. He held onto her shoulders as she walked to her mother's bedroom, took R150 from a cupboard and handed it to the intruder, hoping he would leave. But the man pushed Judith down onto the bed and attempted to rape her. Unable to complete the rape for some unknown reason, he pulled his pants back up, then held the barrel of his gun against the girl's head and pulled the trigger. On his way out, he stole an ATM card which had the PIN written on the back.

Judith's body was discovered by her horrified mother when she returned home later that day.

The eventual identification and arrest of this serial rapist and killer would come as the result of the convergence of a few different lines of investigation, plus the observant nature of the pathologist who performed autopsies on two of the victims.

The list of suspects had been narrowed down by noting which officers had been transferred to the barracks at the time the murders in the area had started. Two names were on that list: 33-year-old Jacques Eksteen and one other officer.

The investigating officer was an experienced detective; his nickname was 'Superhero'. When Superhero began to question Eksteen, he sensed that the man was nervous. His firearm was seized. Superhero noted that the suspect's blood type matched the blood group of the DNA samples taken from some of the scenes. Eksteen's fingerprints were found to be a perfect match to those taken from the scenes, and the young man was arrested on charges of murder, rape and theft.

Eksteen confessed almost immediately to being the serial rapist and murderer who had been terrorising women in the areas around his barracks. He claimed that he felt 'half-relieved' at having been caught. Nonetheless, it emerged that he had taken measures to avoid being apprehended: when the fingerprinting event at the barracks had been conducted, he had purposefully not arrived that day; and, on the day of his arrest, when he heard Superhero was there to interview him, he had swapped out his firearm for the station's 'pool' firearm, which was kept in a safe, in case, he later said, the barrel of his weapon contained physical evidence from the victims he had shot at close range.

After his arrest, a few pieces of the puzzle fell into place, a major one being the murder of Thomasina Selepeng. Thomasina's murder had never been seen as part of this series: she was black, whereas all the other victims were white; and she had been killed in a different area. When the police figured out where Eksteen had previously lived with his parents, however, they realised that his first murder had occurred two years before the 'official' start of the series and that Thomasina had been his first victim.

Eksteen was handed down several life sentences for his crimes and the judge recommended that he never be released back into society.

Jacques' killer story

'Look at his eyes,' says Superhero, across his desk. 'He has snake eyes ....'

Superhero is a capable, serious man. His peers in the Murder and Robbery Squad gave him the nickname following his successful arrest of some of the most notorious criminals of the previous years. The investigating officer who led the investigation into Jacques Eksteen's crimes, who arrested the suspect in his barracks and secured the multiple life sentences, has since left the force for private practice as a fraud investigator. Why? 'I got tired of death. Every day: death.'

Superhero and I are discussing Jacques. Chatting over coffee, we strip back the layers of the case, starting with the simplest: a chronology of Jacques' crimes. Then we run through the list of victims, the escalation of offending.

According to Superhero, Jacques had been a 'good' burglar; one person he stole from claimed there was 'no way that anyone could get into my house'.

Superhero paints an unexpected picture of a man whose crimes held a city in suspense for months, fuelling lurid front pages, with journalists waiting in darkened rooms in his neighbourhood, writing of their fear, and police officers on nearby rooftops.

Jacques, he says, is very open and very honest. 'He spoke a lot to [his] victims; he tried to calm them down. He smoked with one of them, undressing totally ...'

This seeming relaxed intimacy is in stark contrast to the execution of his victims: point-blank gunshots. 'Shit,' I remember mumbling, as I looked at the picture of Jacques' final victim, 'that is cold.' By then I was used to seeing death, but there was something about how the last victim died that spoke of a soul-deep distance.

'Jacques says, "Thank you for catching me," after the arrest,' says Superhero.

'Why?' Superhero asks him.

'Because I couldn't stop killing,' Jacques says.

The next layer is stripped back when I meet Jacques. Surprise has fixed the image in my mind. I had expected someone who looked the part of a police officer-turned-cat burglar and serial mur-derer: imposing, military-neat, muscular. Instead, Jacques shuffles down the corridor shabbily in untied white takkies, looking like a 20-something slacker. A victim's Identikit had been of a face of tough angles, cruel cheekbones; the press had theorised that he was a gymnast, so skilled had his burglaries been. This didn't fit with the shabby stubble and scraggly beard, the slightly sloped, narrow shoulders, and the small, almost feminine hands.

The next layer to be revealed is deeper still, shown in Jacques' incongruous, wry smile at strange times, his deadpan way of speaking, as we sit side by side on a wooden bench sharing pictures of his penpals and eating prison cake. My notes of the time read: 'Feelings [and communicating them] don't seem to impinge on his consciousness, almost as if they are irrelevant. [Jacques] speaks of them as if reading a complex theory he is trying to decipher ...'

I fear that the problem is my lack of skill as an interviewer, or my clunky Afrikaans. In my worry, I call a psychologist who has spoken to Jacques. But he says, 'I noticed this too. He speaks about emotions like someone speaks about cricket when they have never seen the game.'

Despite this, Jacques wants to express his truth: he doesn't allow himself to be prompted by me, correcting me if my reflections or summaries during the interview aren't quite right. He sees the interview as a chance to improve himself: 'It's an education for me; I am bettering myself.'

It is only much later, slogging through transcripts, cross-referencing comments and typing analyses, that I see the patterns emerging from his narrative and catch a glimpse of what Jacques is trying to explain.

Superhero is right about Jacques' eyes, though: they are big and very dark brown, set over a long, prominent nose. They are cold. 'Unless moving,' I note at the time, 'they seem almost dead.'

Jacques' story also comes out in layers: from his public face to his hidden life, and then deeper still, into the darkness he tapped into to survive.

He narrates the facts of his childhood with a shrug of indifference, skimping on detail. Born when apartheid was at its peak, and growing up in the 1980s, Jacques had lived the protected life of many white South Africans at that time. The quiet only child of two normal people, he had a few friends and he took part in the usual social activities for an Afrikaans kid: Voortrekkers, church youth groups, school camps. He played tennis and rugby at school. He didn't fight with his peers. He sometimes forgot homework or chores. He worked hard if he was interested or forced to. He was even a school prefect.

As he tells it, Jacques' childhood was normal to the point of dullness. Even the dramatic events of his childhood are made to sound boring. When he was 10, he spent almost a year in hospital with a 'brain infection, chicken pox, German measles, mumps, had my tonsils removed' – he struggled to remember what illnesses he suffered from – and then had to repeat a year in school. Jacques was unfazed.

The transition to high school, moving to another town, the failure of his family's business, the death of his best friend: all are narrated with an air of dull indifference. The last is the most striking. Jacques says he liked this friend – whose name he doesn't remember – 'more than the others', even staying in touch with him after he moved schools. He had never done that with any friend before, or since. Yet when talking about when that friend died, Jacques shrugs it off with, 'I thought it had to happen some time or another.'

Jacques drifted into adulthood. After graduating from high school, his life appeared directionless. 'I had no idea what I wanted to be, so I just went everywhere to get work. I would do anything. I didn't worry ... I didn't care there wasn't anything I specifically wanted to do, but I would do any work if I was accepted for it.' His lackadaisical attitude may have been justified: before 1994, certain sectors, like policing and the railways, were effectively protected employment for white Afrikaans men. Finding employment wasn't hard.

When Jacques heard that the South African Railways Police (SARP) – which was a separate entity from the South African Police (SAP), and was given the task of guarding the gateways to the country, including railways, airports and harbours – were looking for recruits, he applied. Then he went on holiday. When he returned, he heard that SARP 'still wanted me', so he joined.

Jacques enjoyed his basic training: running, studying, shooting. He enjoyed his assignment to duty in the airports, even travelling abroad, guarding gold shipments, even more. Like at school, his interest is reflected in his achievement: 'At the airport, because I was interested, I wasn't a brilliant policeman, but I did good work.' He even passed his sergeant's exam.

Around the time he was accepted into SARP, Jacques met his future fiancée; he is vague on timings, but thinks they may have met when he was 21. Their relationship lasted the five years leading up to his arrest. This was, as Jacques puts it, his 'first full relationship'.

Jacques, characteristically, never uses his fiancée's name; she is always called 'my fiancée'. Just as characteristically, he meandered into the relationship: an acquaintance became a relationship, and the relationship became a promise of marriage, all without too much effort on Jacques' part.

He describes his fiancée in pleasant terms, and the relationship seems almost devoid of conflict, but beneath it there is a simmering discomfort. Jacques, the disinterested slacker, secretly longed for more. For years, he had been struggling with a sense of isolation, and now the deeper connection promised by an intimate relationship eluded him: 'From both sides, there were times when we didn't talk … there was communication but there wasn't good communication. I maybe expected more.'

With these words, Jacques picks up a theme that has been haunting him since childhood: loneliness.

Jacques lays the blame for this malaise firmly at his parents' door, and his earliest experiences. 'I'm not friends with my parents. [We] never really had a bond.'

His father's character is distant, a faintly ineffectual cardboard cutout. He was, says Jacques

> the sort of person who didn't talk much with me. He worked, he brought the money home, and that's it. He didn't play with you, not with a rugby ball or soccer ball or going fishing or anything like that. [He] wouldn't say, 'Let's go play, just you and me.'

He laments that his father never really paid him attention. His mother, he says, was similarly distant.

> She would make sure I did my homework, and cared for me, bought clothes, and made sure I had food and whatever, [but] there was never really special attention paid, saying, 'How can I help you?' or telling me things about life.

He cannot recall his mother showing him affection during his younger years. His most vivid recollection of her seems to be her discipline. He insists he wasn't abused, though he does say she was strict: 'Scolding, smacks, rough handling.' Any misbehaviour, including not doing homework, led to his being hit, sometimes with a belt. She would want to 'keep me in my place', Jacques reports. She didn't allow him to visit friends' houses alone or go out unsupervised.

Immediately after his initial description of his relationship with his mother and the strict discipline she wielded, Jacques makes the striking statement, 'If you're an only child, you're always lonely.' He blames this on being trapped by the strict discipline of his mother and the seeming indifference of his father. This meant, he says, that '[I] held my frustrations inside, held everything inside, and maybe couldn't communicate.'

> BH: Since you were small, have you always held your
> frustrations inside?
> JE: Ja.
> BH: You didn't communicate with anyone?
> JE: [Quietly] There was no one ...
> BH: On the whole, how did you feel?
> JE: I think I could say I felt alone.

Unable to connect emotionally with parents in turns harsh and distant, Jacques paints himself as an isolated and lonely child. He returns to this image again and again in his story. It comes to represent how he engages with the world.

This perception of isolation had consequences: 'I had problems, but I couldn't discuss them with anyone. I held them inside.' Foremost among these was his struggle with emotions:

> JE: Because I wished myself dead, I cursed myself.
> Through that, I killed my emotions. I didn't know how
> to act out love. It was a difficulty.
> BH: For you, did it always feel like your emotions were
> dead?
> JE: Ja, because I can't ... [struggling to express himself] ...
> know how to handle certain feelings, for example,
> how to be cheerful, or happy. Okay, I knew how to be
> angry, understand, but I can't name all these feelings
> people get. But I know what they are ... Happiness ...
> BH: Or sadness?
> JE: Or to love someone ... I don't know if I got the feelings

33

> [if] I could name them. Having looked at [the feeling]
> on other people's faces, but to live it myself, that's the
> thing.
> BH: So you got these feelings but couldn't live them out?
> JE: Ja ... I don't know how to do emotions.

'Do emotions': the choice of words is striking. To Jacques, emotions are something you act, not something you feel.

Looking back on his life, Jacques is unable to disentangle his isolation from his inability to fully experience emotion. Did one cause or the other? Were they separate issues? Were his parents to blame, or was it his fault? How could he break the invisible walls around him, that cycle of isolation and dissatisfaction?

We stumbled on the answer to the last question quite suddenly in his interview, while discussing his childhood loneliness. He was mentioning the limitation of his friendships around the age of 12:

> [I] didn't discuss personal things with [other same-aged
> children], like for example, 'I like that girl and would like to
> go out with her' or 'I took money from my mom's bag, let's
> go and buy sweets', something like that. If you feel alone,
> then you can take money from your mother's handbag and
> go to the cafe and play [arcade] games on the machines,
> that sort of thing. If you can't go to a friend, you must make
> your own amusement.

And, just like that, Jacques' story creates the link between loneliness and crime: stealing brought him relief from loneliness. Again and again, Jacques' thefts gave him relief from loneliness, from his inability to express emotions.

> BH: Did it feel good for you, the theft?
> JE: Ja. It's fun. It was an adventure. You're enjoying
> yourself. You've got money to waste or whatever. You
> didn't work for that ... It wasn't planned.
> BH: You just thought, 'I've got money, it's good'?
> JE: Ja. The stealing from the handbags was fun, I can say
> that.

These seemingly petty childhood thefts were profoundly significant for Jacques:

> I didn't perceive that what I was doing by stealing out the handbag was a problem, and that it can get bigger.

He returns to his thefts repeatedly in his story, particularly when asked about the reasons for the worst of his crimes.

At one point, I ask him whether he suffers from nightmares. His answer is telling:

> No, I don't. But I do think about the things that I've done; it comes back to me a lot. Like, for example, okay, when I think back to the woman I shot in the bath. It just comes into my thoughts. I don't look to think about it, you understand, because it will always stay with me. I think back about the times I stole money from handbags, that comes very often. It comes, not every day, but it comes often.

The smooth, incongruous segue from talking about a murder he committed to talking about stealing from handbags is noteworthy. Jacques is pained by the hindsight of where his thieving adventures would lead.

As his sense of isolation deepened, so did his need for criminal adventures. Just as Jacques started a relationship and became a police officer, he began burgling houses.

> BH: What made you decide to enter [and steal from] a house for the first time?
>
> JE: Okay, um, I can't remember what made me decide to do this. As I said, maybe it was an impulse. It wasn't a decision that I sat down and took: 'Okay, now I'm going to break into a house!' I just saw: the window's open, the opportunity is there; I'd go in.

The first few times, he just stole money.

> JE: I'd go in to get cash. There are people there. Men, women, children and whatnot. I just went in and opened the handbag and took cash, where it was in the bedroom or so on.

BH: Was it at night?

JE: At night, but [the people were] not sleeping. They were busy eating or watching TV or whatever. A couple of times I was busy and people came in and they saw me, then I made tracks.

BH: Did you ever attack anyone to get away?

JE: No.

BH: After the time, did you feel excited, with the adrenalin, from the thrill of it?

JE: [Pause] I couldn't say. I couldn't swear by it. You can say I was scared someone would catch me, or whatever, when I began. But eventually you don't worry. It becomes a habit, and you just do it because it's lekker [fun].

In sharp contrast to the passivity in other areas of his life, Jacques' character when offending was impulsive, goal-oriented, decisive. He describes keeping watch on houses, entering swiftly, quickly stealing items and then escaping. 'At first you worry, but soon you don't,' he says.

Things rapidly escalated. Jacques gives a confused and stuttering account of a seeing a woman alone in a house and deciding to try to rape her.

BH: Was this near your parents' house?

JE: Ja, just over the street, diagonally across. There is no special reason I want to rape women, you understand. I just thought, 'Why [don't] I do this?' Maybe I enjoyed it, because you do it secretly. You enjoy doing it, the sneakiness, no one knows about it [speaks faster, in a more excited tone] to be sneaky, to sneak around at night, to search for money. Then you come to the stage where you see there's a woman, you see through the window that there's one body on the bed, so you go through the window and pull the duvet off. But you don't have the wherewithal to know what to do next, then she screams, and you run away.

Note how Jacques expresses satisfaction that this behaviour was secret and separate, because at this stage in his story, he was alone.

His parents, his fiancée, faded from his narrative. No new friends are named. No-one but Jacques himself existed in his inner world. With this, the scene was set for his first murder.

Jacques never refers to the people he killed by their names. He calls the murders 'incidents', the dispassionate language of a police docket.

His description of the murder of Thomasina Selepeng is shambolic. In contrast to his usually precise descriptions, his account of her death is jumbled and unclear. It reflects the confusion of a burglar who entered looking for money, and suddenly found events spiralling out of control.

Thomasina's killing was impulsive, almost accidental. He had entered her room driven by confused impulses and narratives. But her murder planted the seeds of new options in his search for adventure. Jacques never considered raping someone before this, but

> maybe after the first incident, I did begin to think about
> rape. I thought I would try rape a woman, if I saw her there,
> and she looked nice.

It was almost two years, though, before Jacques committed his first rape. In the interim, he 'went back to stealing money'. Jacques had built a narrative that helped him commit burglary and theft. It did not yet provide him with justification for rape and murder.

Then Jacques' career took a turn for the worse. The SARP were disbanded and its members were incorporated into the SAP. Jacques was moved into the Riot Squad. This meant he was policing the townships at the height of the anti-apartheid unrest in the late 1980s and early 1990s. The newsreels from that time are harrowing: angry crowds, floating clouds of smoke or teargas, the popping of automatic weapons or the boom of shotguns, people scattering for their lives or lying in the carelessly dropped attitudes of the dead. Jacques' only comment, in an indifferent tone, is 'people shot at us, threw stones and petrol bombs'. He then complains that 'you always worked in the same place and did the same things'; the quality of his work was 'not so good', he added. In this tumult, Jacques was bored.

Jacques' wedding was then postponed following a disagreement with his father-in-law. This, too, he met with indifference.

Too deeply isolated to reach, indifferent to his potential marriage, trapped in what he saw as a boring and repetitive job, Jacques moved into the police barracks in a residential suburb and seemed to slip seamlessly back into his adolescent life. He does not report having any problem fitting in.

He quickly lost touch with the friends he had made at college and during previous postings, saying:

> You just get other friends. I'm not the sort of person who says, 'He's my friend, I'll go with him or stay in touch.' If he goes, he goes. It doesn't bother me.

He says he spent most of his time on his own, finding nothing unusual or unpleasant in this.

There is an irony in Jacques' indifference to companions and relationships, an indifference that coexists alongside his resentment at his loneliness and isolation. Perhaps he was too locked into his search for adventure to escape. Perhaps, as in his youth, isolating himself from others gave him the freedom to steal in peace. He himself comments on this split, saying that his offences were almost not part of his normal life:

> I was two people. One was violent and the other was soft natured, or whatever. I'm the same person, I just have two sides: one good side and one bad side that no one knows about apart from me.

The SAP unwittingly supplied Jacques' 'bad side' with a frightening assistant. The Vektor Z88 is a South African copy of one of the most popular combat pistols in the world. Matte black and chunky, it propels a 9 mm lump of lead at 380 metres per second. It was also the SAP's standard pistol. Jacques' move into the Riot Squad's barracks meant that he got one to keep.

> BH: At what stage did you know, if I find a woman, I'll rape her?
> JE: When I got the weapon, it gave me the strength to do

> this thing: if I get a woman, I'll rape her. When I could
> take the pistol home, that gave me strength to do
> things, to stand there and say, 'I'm here to rape you.' I
> wouldn't do it without the weapon.

Refuting any other motive or cause, Jacques says he took the next step and committed rape simply because his gun made it easy for him to do so.

Jacques describes the rape of Sylvia Claassen with a precision and clarity missing from his account of the murder of Thomasina Selepeng. This clarity matches the confidence and calmness of his actions. His internal story changed with this rape. The 'sneakiness' and 'fun' of thefts gained another layer: the desire for experience. Hidden in this desire, there seems to have been a deeper yearning, as if the experience of rape would fulfil Jacques in some way: 'you're looking for something in the sexual act ...'

> The first time was just a reaction. The second one, I got
> feelings. I had the firearm; now, I can go and do it. After that, I
> wanted to do it again; couldn't control myself, the feeling to do
> it again. I was in a cycle and couldn't get out, that's why I did
> it again. Like, I enjoyed stealing handbags, [so] you feel you
> want to do it again. The excitement brought me to doing it.
> The sneaking around to rape, maybe to experiment, to find out
> how it feels to rape or ejaculate inside a woman. I'm searching
> for something, and I don't know what it is, so I go on and on. I
> know it wasn't lust, or because I hate women; it wasn't taking
> my frustrations out on women. I just enjoyed the stealing and
> the sneaking around, and I couldn't tear myself free of it.

He knew we would be caught: his offences were causing panic in the largely middle-class suburban area around the barracks, and newspaper headlines splashed fear through the neighbourhood, drawing a strong police response.

> JE: After the third incident they put policemen on the roof.
> Okay, I heard it, but it didn't bother me. I knew they
> were looking for me. And when I went back to the
> barracks, if someone spoke about it, I didn't talk,
> I just listened. I wasn't worried. Maybe, already,

> I hoped they would catch me. I knew that they would
> catch me some time.

BH: You already knew this?

JE: Yes, I knew this. I knew I wouldn't always be able to
get away with it. It was definitely a solution that they
must catch me. That's why I didn't wear gloves, I didn't
wipe out fingerprints or many marks. I knew they
would catch me, but I couldn't stop myself.
I didn't get advice or talk to anyone. At that stage
I didn't know I couldn't stop, but later I realised that
I would never have stopped.

Isolated and self-involved, Jacques was caught up in the habit of rape: the increasing confidence, the arrogant indifference towards the victims, the thrill. He says his sleep patterns changed to accommodate his offending. He would carry out reconnaissance at around 8 pm, then return home and sleep. He'd wake later, have a coffee and 'go find someone to rape'.

Jacques rushed full-flight from rape to murder when he shot Rebecca Strydom. It is tempting to see his cold-blooded killing of Rebecca as a milestone or a point of change. Not for Jacques. To most people, there is something uniquely horrifying about the act of killing another, extinguishing a life, but in Jacques, this horror is absent. Nor does he delight in it, as other murderers have done.

> I don't think I felt anything about it. To kill is just to kill. I didn't
> do it to experiment, I just did it because the light was on.

From this point on, Jacques would murder simply to protect his identity.

Two weeks later, Jacques raped and murdered Belinda Wiley. He arrived armed with all his criminal confidence, the intimidation of his words and his weapon, to control her as much as he could have wished. He spent longer with her, in complete control. Here, the act of rape continued for the longest time of all his victims. All his crimes had been building up to this chance to commit what he later admitted was the crime he enjoyed most. He comments coyly, smiling, 'It's almost as if you know her.' 'Almost', but not really; not enough.

Given complete control, he didn't know what to do once the rape was completed. Jacques can't quite explain why he asked Belinda to have a bath, or why he shared a cigarette with her. Maybe he was hoping that this experience would help him finally break out of his isolation. Maybe he was feeling the same regret an addict feels when they find out that not even a massive dose of their chosen drug can ease their loneliness.

Whatever the reason, the cool, confident offender started to fall apart after Belinda's murder. The words Jacques uses to describe his crimes change at this point: he talks less about fun and adventure and more about habit:

> It was fun to steal from handbags. But as it goes on, it's a habit that you learnt; you can't stop. You want to do it more and more; you can't control it. You do it more, as a habit. I didn't think at that stage that it was nice and exciting, an adventure or whatever, I just did it. Maybe it was out of habit or because I couldn't control myself.

Confused, perhaps by the changes within him, there was a pause of five months before he killed Margaret Welwyn. In that crime, Jacques fired his gun at the first sign of resistance. He thought about rape but didn't go through with it.

The killing of his final victim, 16-year-old Judith Schoeman, followed the same pattern: a failed attempt at rape and then shooting the victim dead.

The calmness and control of his previous offences was gone. He offended during the day, becoming 'reckless'. He even seemed to revert to earlier habits: using physical violence to control his victims and still, just like when he was young, stealing money.

The last two murders saw Jacques' attitude towards his victims change. He was always indifferent to his victims, but now this had sharpened to thinly veiled contempt. He killed Margaret as soon as she began struggling and smirked in amusement at the incongruous injury his gunshot had caused.

Judith's murder had an even more chilling touch. When a gun is pressed against a bony surface and fired, it creates a distinct wound, caused by the ignition gases bursting the skin into a four-pointed star. Judith had this star in the middle of her forehead. This can only mean that Jacques leant over her, pressed his heavy automatic pistol into her forehead, face to face, and pulled the trigger. Nothing can express his profound isolation better. It's as if, in discovering that rape did not cure his isolation and loneliness, for him, his victims became completely disposable, less even than objects for experimentation.

Jacques had never bothered taking measures to avoid forensic detection. He'd never taken away cartridge cases or wiped away fingerprints. He recalls sitting in the barracks after his offences, worrying about all the things that could lead to his capture. Yet, when it came, Jacques accepted his arrest with the characteristic passivity he brought to his daily life

> I was half glad when they caught me. I knew I could never give up. It was like a drug that you had to have more and more. You just go forward. You don't know where you're going. You don't have control, you don't think about it, you just go on.

As Jacques reflects, so should we. It's impossible to know whether his struggle to understand emotions was something he was born with, something that grew as a result of his environment, or a bit of both. What is clear is that it created a dynamic with his emerging loneliness; it became his inner story. Jacques' thievery started as a response to his sense of loneliness and emotional isolation. In contrast to the mundane events of his normal life, crime provided thrills and adventure. Those thrills became addictive, pulling him unknowingly down a path to far worse crimes.

Loneliness was not just the spark that lit this dark fire, however. By isolating Jacques from others, it clouded his eyes to the downward path under his feet. It meant his emotional distance became an unbridgeable gulf between him and the world.

The poignant image of Jacques as a lonely child is compelling. Who wouldn't feel a flicker of pity for a child trying to find his way in a confusing world, unhelped by cold and distant parents? Who doesn't twinge in empathy with a teenager finding the world of emotions confusing and incomprehensible? Who doesn't fear the spectre of loneliness creeping into their life?

There is something different about Jacques' loneliness, though. He was trapped by loneliness, as we all sometimes are – but he started to relish it. Speaking about his isolation at high school, he acknowledges that 'I should have done something about it, but I didn't'. Instead of directly addressing it, he embraced the crimes he committed to cope with it. He accepted loneliness as inevitable, and, in doing so, freed himself of any obligation to other people.

In the isolation it brought, he was free to pursue his growing addiction to theft and rape. In this isolation, all internal controls over him were removed. He became ever more self-interested, self-involved. He had no obligation to others. Loneliness became a freedom to do whatever he wanted.

This is the second killer story: loneliness as a freedom from obligation, isolation in a world of you.

3 Sisanda: Revenge

The crimes

In mid-1994, the body of a young woman was discovered at a rural Eastern Cape bus stop. Detectives arriving at the scene soon determined that she had not been killed there: the bus stop was nothing more than a body-disposal site.

The victim, who would later be identified as a young police officer, Stella Mogotsi, had marks around her neck which at autopsy would attribute the cause of death to ligature strangulation. Strangulation by ligature differs from manual strangulation in that the offender uses an object such as a piece of rope or wire to restrict air flow, rather than their hands, forearm or other limb. Stella's service weapon was missing.

Three years later, 200 kilometres away in another town, the body of another young woman was found at a bus depot. The body had been wrapped in a plastic bag and a floral sheet. A pair of pantyhose was still tied around her neck and the autopsy confirmed that she had indeed been strangled to death. She had also been raped. Her cellphone was missing. She would be identified only much later.

The following month, Sihle Tana's 15-year-old daughter, Zondi, went missing. The girl had gone to visit her mother and had not been seen since then. Sihle searched for his daughter for days, and eventually, almost two weeks later, he discovered her body in an empty apartment. The girl had been raped, tied to a chair and strangled with a nylon rope.

The discovery of Zondi's body set in motion the chain of events necessary to unmask a serial killer.

Sihle Tana was a detective with the SAPS. Despite being overwhelmed by the tragedy of losing his young daughter in such a horrific way, his investigative instincts kicked in and he soon identified a person he believed could be responsible for her murder.

Sisanda Mandlenkosi was Zondi's stepfather. He had married her mother, Sihle's ex-wife, Thembeni, when Zondi was relatively young, but Sihle knew that the marriage was on the rocks. Sisanda didn't live with the family full time and, like many South Africans, had to spend large periods of time away from home in order to find work. Sisanda usually returned home during the school holidays to spend time with his wife and Sihle knew that the period during which Zondi had been abducted and murdered coincided with one of Sisanda's visits.

Sihle also knew that Thembeni had intended to tell Sisanda that she wanted a divorce during this time, and that she expected an explosive reaction to the news.

Sihle reported this to his superior at the SAPS and an investigation was soon underway.

One of the first things police discovered when they began to dig into Sisanda's background was that Thembeni had not been the only woman in his life. His transience had meant that he had been able to keep several girlfriends in different areas. He would later admit that his wife had discovered his infidelity and that this was the reason she'd decided to divorce him.

In an effort to better understand their suspect and his behaviour, investigators made contact with the landlord at his last known place of residence, a woman called Nandi. Nandi turned out to have quite an established connection to Sisanda Mandlenkosi: she had been the second wife of his deceased brother.

She offered investigators information about Sisanda, including that she had asked him to pack his belongings and leave because he was not paying his rent on time and she wanted to rent the space out to someone else. Her brother-in-law had not taken the news well, she said. Then she mentioned something that piqued the police's curiosity: her friend Portia Mashabela, who had been living with her and Sisanda on the same premises, had inexplicably disappeared, and her disappearance had coincided with Sisanda's eviction.

The detective investigating Zondi Tana's murder now suspected that he might have a serial offender on his hands. A warrant of arrest was issued for Sisanda, but it became clear that the man was on the run. Eventually a R50 000 reward would be issued for information leading to his arrest.

Soon afterwards, Nandi made two discoveries that would link Sisanda to even more crimes: a suitcase containing clothing that she did not recognise in the garage at her home, and then a firearm hidden in her house.

The suitcase would be linked to a case of attempted murder that had been opened earlier that year, when Paulina Mbuli had walked into a police station and told police officers that a man who had been giving her a lift had attacked her and attempted to strangle her, and that when she struck him in the genitals, he had pushed her out of the vehicle and driven away with her suitcase.

The suitcase Nandi found in her garage belonged to Paulina Mbuli. Sisanda had been her attacker.

The firearm Nandi found was a SAPS service weapon that had been issued to Stella Mogotsi, the female police officer whose body had been found at the bus stop. Now, detectives were able to uncover another important link: Stella had been a girlfriend of Sisanda.

An unsolved rape and attempted murder case dating back a year proved to be Sisanda's first crime – a trial run, perhaps, for his murders. He had given a lift to the teenage daughter of a family friend and along the way he had pulled over on the side of the road and attacked her. He had strangled her until she had lost consciousness, then he raped her. He had then taken her to a nearby house, where he had tried to rape her again. The girl had fought back and managed to escape, and had sought the assistance of a nearby homeowner.

By the time Sisanda was eventually arrested and brought to trial, a fourth murder had been added to his charge sheet: a Methodist minister's wife had been found raped and strangled to death on the one evening her husband had not been at home and the friend who usually stayed with her had also not been present. The woman's husband had always suspected Sisanda, who was carrying out handyman tasks at the man's property at the time, but no clear effort had been made to investigate his suspicions.

Sisanda was found guilty of all charges except the murder of the minister's wife. He was handed down several long prison sentences, including a life sentence for the murder of Zondi Tana.

Sisanda's killer story

The maximum-security prison is a long, low series of buildings, hunched into the sea winds. Sisanda and I are sitting in the familiar interview room, with a barred window looking out into the blue sky above the coastal flats.

Sisanda cuts a neat figure, tidily dressed in green prison fatigues, with a red-and-white AIDS awareness badge on the left pocket of his shirt; tall, with a shaved head, apart from two missing teeth, he is unmarked by the violence in his life. Friendly and non-confrontational, he sits still in his chair, quiet and calm, speaking good English softly but confidently.

Sisanda is easily hurt. The hurt appears on his face when I ask questions that seem threatening. He becomes upset when I first mention his murders. Maybe he does not want to reflect deeply on his emotions and motivations. Maybe he can't: even discussing a strong negative emotion seems hard for him. When I ask him a question about an emotional topic, he stops and thinks through his answer before eventually replying, his voice quiet.

Soon I can tell from this 'emotional pause' how much emotion a question stirs up for Sisanda. With less threatening questions, he sits back in his chair, with his head resting on the upright, then half-closes his eyes and looks at me out of the bottom of them. If the question evokes stronger emotions, he breaks eye contact and looks at the door or the floor, staring into nothing, lapsing into silence or giving curt answers.

In prison, as in life, some people are very concerned with portraying themselves as socially acceptable or admirable. Despite his struggle with emotions, Sisanda isn't one of them. He paints a believable picture of himself as a flawed and human figure, and I like him for it. I enjoy his tendency to joke about his life, his disarming honesty and self-deprecation, even more. That is why, in a pause in the interview while the tape recorder is switched off, I happen to ask Sisanda, 'What's your favourite place in the world? Where would you like to be?'

He looks out the window across the flats and says, 'Cape Town. I'd love to see Cape Town.'

I feel a twinge of sadness at the melancholic optimism of this answer. With four murder convictions, I doubt he'll see the outside of a prison again before he dies, much less feel the Cape wind on his face.

As any storyteller will tell you, one of the great sources of energy and vitality in any narrative are the characters. Just like people look at the clouds and see monsters or castles or shapes, if no characters exist in a story, we humans will imaginatively transform inanimate objects to do this job. We personalise our universe. It may be why so many different schools of psychology have used the concept of an inner character to explain how humans behave and are motivated.

While the various schools of psychology agree that our inner characters are powerful motivators for our behaviours, they see the characters as different representations: of somebody you know, of yourself, or of different parts of yourself. The names also change, with terms like 'imago', 'mythic persona' and 'inner self' all referring to one or more of these representations.

So, what does it mean to have characters in your internal story?

In every story, the characters have a purpose. Let's start with the idea of the characters being a representation of someone else. Think of the idea of a person that pops into your head when you hear their name: Mom, Dad, significant other. These characters are obviously not the actual person, copied into your skull. Rather, they are an inner representation of that person's most important characteristics. This simplifies the person, exaggerating some characteristics, missing out others, focusing on what that person means to you.

Your inner characters can also be representations of yourself, or parts of yourself. Think of the person you are when you're enjoying yourself with friends versus the person you are when you walk into a tough work meeting. In your inner narrative, it's likely that these two characters look, speak and behave differently.

Whoever they are associated with, the inner characters share a purpose in our stories: they represent how people behave in the world. Our stories use characters to represent ways of behaving towards others. This helps us navigate through life. Our characters become an inner guide to how to operate in the world and in relation to other people. This inner guide has the potential to influence the way we behave in real life.

We intuitively recognise the power of these internal characters in our stories: just look at all the cartoons of people with an angel on one shoulder and the devil on the other, whispering in their ears, battling for control.

A 1997 study of the narratives of violent offenders found, like my study, that people who commit violent acts have violent internal characters. The study's author, Lonnie Athens, used the evocative term 'phantom others' for these inner characters. As in our killer stories, these phantom others were created as the offenders inter- acted with the people around them and helped them to make sense of the world around them. As in our killer stories, the more violent the phantom others, the more violent the crimes that person would be likely to commit.

Athens, though, adds something extra to our killer stories, in the imagery he uses of a 'phantom community'. He found that the various phantom others interact with each other, and that the person interacts with this community, without their always being aware of doing so. The image of a phantom community, whispering darkness into our mind, is a powerful one. The secret stories we tell ourselves are sometimes even secrets to ourselves.

I use the concept of inner characters as a tool to explain how the inner stories of serial murderers develop and how these inner stories are then reflected in their crimes. Let's see how they are revealed in Sisanda's story.

Sisanda's story is one of strange ambiguity, a series of contradictions. Imagine it as the opening sequence to a film. The opening shot is a wide-angle landscape one: the rumpled, rolling hills of the Eastern Cape, dusty beige and green beneath a vast blue sky. Small villages, towns and townships are scattered among the valleys. The distance between them, the vast scale of the landscape, creates an impression of timeless rural peace.

It's a false impression. It's the 1980s, the dying years of apartheid, and the townships are racked with violence. Smoke and the smell of burnt rubber hangs over the rooftops. Police and political factions struggle for dominance in a vicious cycle of protest, armed battle and covert killing.

Sisanda's recollections of this time 'are of houses burning, people being harassed, things like that'. One day, at school, Sisanda and his peers were led from class by older youths and ordered to abandon learning and join the protests. When he questioned this, Sisanda was smashed into unconsciousness with a rock.

Zoom in again, and there's another contrast: Sisanda in the bosom of his family, the 'only place I felt safe'. His eldest sister is his main caregiver, 'loving and caring'. His eldest brother is idolised, an emblem of all Sisanda wants to be. Sisanda describes his family as his only friends until he was an adult.

Zoom out slightly. While at school, he describes his main hobby as fighting with the other kids, while home appears to be a picture of cosy domesticity. 'The only place I felt comfortable,' says Sisanda, 'was playing at home in the yard.'

Zoom in again, though, and Sisanda is describing how his sister would discipline him terribly and beat him if he didn't listen. He tells how his childhood was largely nomadic as he was moved from relative to relative, cutting a lonely figure in a hostile landscape ...

So, the layered story of Sisanda's life unfolds, each layer not quite matching the one before. To understand it, to find a route through the contradictions, let's slow down the film. Let's focus on the one feature of his story that shows clear patterns: the characters. In Sisanda's story of himself, how does he represent himself and other people? What do these inner representations tell us about how Sisanda came to commit his crimes?

The story of Sisanda's childhood was dominated by three characters: the Lonely Child, the Happy Family and the Elder Brother.

Sisanda introduces his eldest brother in the first five minutes of our interview. 'I wanted to be what he was,' he says. 'I couldn't compare him to anyone else. I put him in a higher place to other people.' He lists his brother's attributes and interests: emotionally contained, being a church minister, good with his hands and able to fix anything.

His eldest brother's characteristics and skills become integrated into the character of the Elder Brother in Sisanda's internal narrative. This character provides Sisanda with an internal source of inspiration, an elder providing wisdom and guidance.

Listening to Sisanda describing his brother, though, something else becomes obvious: Sisanda doesn't talk about his brother's emotional life, what his brother thought or felt. His inner character of the Elder Brother is consistently presented as always positive, essentially one-dimensional.

Sisanda's next character is that of the Happy Family. Sisanda describes his family as warm, close and communal; he goes so far as presenting them as the only source of solace and friendship as he was growing up – so much so that he made his first friend from outside the family only when he was 24 years old.

It thus comes as a surprise that he can't recall many pleasant memories from a childhood he describes as 'nice' and 'very good'. Instead, he remembers how his mother and eldest sister would 'discipline me terribly', hitting him when he was asleep; and how both his parents were heavy drinkers, and never around. In contrast to the communal warmth he describes, he says he was moved from house to house, shifted every time his relatives struggled to handle his behaviour.

This ambiguity of the Happy Family character becomes embedded in Sisanda's story of himself.

When he was eight years old, unrest swept the townships. Three years later, his parents died. Sisanda shies away from describing this, saying he wasn't upset, as they were 'not so close'.

Despite his words, Sisanda later admits that he twice attempted suicide. He was around '10 or 11' years old.

SM: [Quiet, hesitant] I never told my family. I took gas.
     Instead of killing me, it made my tummy run. [Laughs]
BH: What made you want to kill yourself?
SM: I was lonely. I felt lonely there.
BH: Did you feel like your parents had, sort of, rejected you
     by dying?
SM: I felt that God was horrible to me. God gave this thing
     to me. It didn't feel like God was there. I had to be
     angry at God. He was rejecting me; God was pushing
     me away from him.
BH: Did you always believe in God?
SM: Yes.

The third and most important character of his childhood was the Lonely Child.

BH: Did you ever feel lonely when you were growing up?
SM: Yes. Even today I get lonely.
BH: And what's that loneliness like?
SM: To me, to be lonely ... [Sighs, pauses] It's like, eeh,
     when you see it seems as if people are looking away,
     they don't want to come near you. That makes me
     feel very lonely. Especially if I like to say something
     to you, and then I see that you are pushing me away
     from you. That makes me feel bad.
BH: And did that happen, has that happened a lot to you?
SM: Yes.
BH: And is loneliness close to rejection for you?
SM: Ja.
BH: Do you get angry with that?
SM: [Pauses, sighs] A lot.

I notice an association between Sisanda's loneliness, his feeling of rejection, and anger. When I push him on this, he falls into silence, so I try another tack.

> BH: What do you do when you're angry?
> SM: When I'm angry ... If you made me angry, to me, for that anger to go away, I have to get hold of you. I have to touch you. Whether to hit you once or you hit me, but I hate it when someone makes me angry, then goes away without me having to touch him or having a fight with that particular person. For that anger to go away, I have to do something to you.

This pattern of loneliness, rejection and violence is the crucible that forged the Lonely Child. Like his other characters, the Lonely Child became an inner guide to Sisanda to how to operate in the world and in relation to other people. It most closely represents the violent response and the hate of rejection that he returns to repeatedly when he describes himself.

Sisanda's relationships with his peers seemed to consist solely of getting into fights with them.

> SM: To me, having a fight is nothing. Then I can say something to you, then you get angry, then I would not apologise. I would just push you or hit you for the wrong that I have done to you. I used to be like that.
> BH: Did you get in lots of fights?
> SM: Yes. Fighting for me was like a hobby. [Laughs]

Sisanda's descriptions of the idyllic family life of his youth appear at odds with the death, violence and sense of loneliness and rejection he also describes in his childhood. Perhaps the Lonely Child became the character into which he poured all the negativity of his youth. This meant the Elder Brother and the Happy Family could continue to be sources of pure inspiration and comfort.

Moreover, the Lonely Child gave Sisanda control. It allowed him to control the horrible feelings of loneliness that swelled whenever he thought someone was rejecting him. The Lonely Child, through Sisanda, learnt to control this through anger and revenge: 'For that anger to go away, I have to get hold of you.' In his search for acceptance, this pattern haunted Sisanda's footsteps.

Growing into his teenage years, the narratives of Sisanda's life started to split, mirroring the isolation between his main characters.

> What I can say is that I developed late, you see. Other boys, they started doing things, smoking and having girls, at the age of 13, 14. But I liked to play, just play alone, doing wire cars and all that stuff. So I developed late. Maybe I developed after 17 years, then I started to have a friend then, you see.

Sisanda would play truant from school, longing to 'sit at home and do nothing' in the solace of his family. With disarming honesty, he describes himself as lazy, only making an effort at school when sent to another city to live with his eldest brother.

In the hesitant tone that he uses to describe emotional events, he describes that once he was there with his brother, 'everything changed': his schoolwork improved, and he says he was 'happy with people'.

Unfortunately, when Sisanda returned to the Eastern Cape, his behaviour lapsed. The Lonely Child depended on the character of the Elder Brother to keep it in check.

In sharp contrast, however, is how Sisanda describes his attitude towards 'the Struggle' (as the fight against apartheid became known) and his role in it. Here, his character becomes more like that of the Elder Brother: intellectual, principled. Although he disliked the township fighting that embroiled his community, he became a political advisor to local ANC-affiliated comrades.

> SM: Some of them [community members], they were stupid, who did bad things. They didn't follow the politics. They didn't read books and all that stuff. I like to read in books.
>
> BH: You did it for the politics; they did it because they liked to break things?
>
> SM: Break things and all that stuff, ja.

Sisanda shunned indiscriminate violence and said he would only take part in violence if it could be proven that his target was 'the system'. The desired characteristics and aspirations of the Elder Brother were being brought into his own life.

Another evolution in his inner characters occurred as Sisanda's teenage years approached their end. He describes the first time he had sex, aged 18, as 'the nicest thing I ever had'. His first love, Sweetie, again 'changed everything'. She was older than Sisanda, took him under her wing, 'taught me how to love'.

For a while it seemed as if Sisanda would reach those dreams of warmth and acceptance that the Happy Family always seemed to promise but never quite deliver. Their relationship lasted three years. Then, catastrophe.

> SM: She broke my heart. She fell for another man.
> BH: How did that make you feel?
> SM: [Long pause] To me, I wanted to revenge. I wanted to do something to her for what she had done to me, but I didn't have the guts to do it. There was something, there was a way of getting her, of hurting her; but then I didn't have the guts to do [it]. I wanted to hurt her. Hurt her. Whether it was going to be physically or any other way I could try.

Sisanda's words ominously foreshadow what was to come, and he whispers 'yes' when I ask whether rejection was the worst thing he could suffer, the thing most deserving of revenge.

This marked the birth of a character of the Vengeful Lover. The Vengeful Lover is what the Lonely Child grew into. The Lonely Child's longing for acceptance and hatred of rejection was woven into the fabric of this new, adult character.

This new character gave Sisanda another way of overcoming those negative emotions: intimate relationships and sex. This was the 'lover'. Unfortunately, the event that gave birth to the lover also gave the anger of the Lonely Child a focus: the women who rejected him. This is the 'vengeful' aspect.

Where previously the Lonely Child was unable to overcome the loneliness and rejection it feared, the Vengeful Lover provided

Sisanda two means of doing this: through intimate relationships which evoked the acceptance of his Happy Family character, and through revenge to overcome any subsequent rejection.

The Vengeful Lover swiftly became the dominant character in Sisanda's narrative. In so doing, it sowed the seeds of a lethal dynamic in his inner story, deepening the split between the positive and the negative characters.

At first glance, though, Sisanda seemed committed to using this character as an enjoyable focus in his life, and embarked on an adventurous, prolific love life. He estimates that he had sex with more than 50 women, saying he came to prefer women 10 to15 years older than him, like Sweetie was. He developed the habit of 'proposing' to women he was acquainted with; that is, proposition-ing them for sex.

Sisanda reports having been sexually adventurous and enjoying experimentation with partners and prostitutes. No violence filtered into these experiments, though – none of the bondage you may expect if you read books on serial murder.

Sisanda enjoyed pornography and kept a collection of books and videos. He reports having had a girlfriend who worked in a sex shop, and on being asked whether he enjoyed visiting the sex shop, he replied, '[I] had no choice. She worked there. I had better like it,' and laughed.

After school, alongside his colourful love life, Sisanda appears to have maintained a conventional and modestly successful life. He held various odd jobs in the two years it took him to obtain a professional electrician's qualification. He married the year after, by which time he was working as a machine operator. His wife, Thembeni, is left nameless for much of his narrative.

Sisanda liked work, enjoying working fast and doing things properly. He cheerfully reports that his love for hard work got him into trouble with some bosses, who feared he would make them look bad by comparison. But he was never fired, and modestly assesses himself as a 'fair' worker.

A year after his marriage, Sisanda opened his own subcontract-ing electrical firm and worked on both municipality houses and private jobs until his arrest three years later. He describes his work life honestly, saying that there were times when his business did not go well, but that overall there were 'no big problems'.

Behind his modest assessment, a key character of his adulthood was being born. The Good Family Man was educated, making a success of his business, was hard working, and had even got married. This character's purpose was to encapsulate everything positive and aspirational in the character of the Elder Brother and bring it into Sisanda's story.

Doing this, of course, helped boost Sisanda's positive sense of self. Previously, he'd had to rely on the physical presence of his eldest brother to keep his behaviour in check or help him focus on work; now, this internal character took on this role. The Good Family Man protected the positive aspects of Sisanda's personality from the effect of the more chaotic elements of his lifestyle. It also allowed Sisanda to continue to consider himself a good family man, while simultaneously living the life of the Vengeful Lover.

Sisanda is uncomfortable when our conversation brings together the worlds of the Vengeful Lover and the Good Family Man, such as happens when I ask whether his wife knew about his affairs. After a long, emotional pause, he shamefacedly whispers, 'Yes.'

It takes a while to travel between towns and villages in the rugged rurality of the Eastern Cape. You'll spend most of your time bouncing along winding roads through the rolling shrug of the landscape, before suddenly rounding a shoulder of land and seeing below you the sprawl of a township, plunging into the bustle of a larger rural town, or rolling into the sleepy suburbs of one of the cities. It's easy to imagine Sisanda as a carefree Casanova in this landscape, rattling from town to town, a woman waiting for him in every destination, the sun streaming through his car windows. The semi-nomadic lifestyle of his childhood seemed now to suit him.

This imagined ideal masks the growing darkness in his story, the darkness sown in the events that gave birth to the Vengeful Lover. Since Sweetie, his first love, Sisanda had been extremely sensitive to rejection by women. Although he was subsequently rejected only three times, and each relationship lasted less than a year, he states, 'I felt that rejection. I hated it.'

BH: Would you say that's the thing you hated most?
SM: Yes.

He repeats the names of the girls who rejected him, pausing emotionally between each. Even though he was promiscuous, Sisanda is jealous towards the many women he was involved with, a fact he admits is not logical:

For me, it's easier to be in love with a number of girls. But I hate it when a girl does the same thing to me, to share me with somebody else, you see? She must not share me. But to me, I am doing that. [Laughs]

Sisanda's response to rejection did not change with age. Just as the Lonely Child was violent, so was the Vengeful Lover. The Vengeful Lover's violence was more focused, though. To this character, the women associated with the Rejecting Woman character in Sisanda's inner story deserved the violence meted out to them. These women become the sole focus of Sisanda's violence.

The Vengeful Lover soon developed a routine, a preferred pattern for violence: 'I liked to kick. Once, twice, and then leave it.' Sisanda didn't need to hurt the women badly, just enough to show his dominance, his control.

Talking about his reasons for being violent towards partners who argued with him, he says, 'I wanted to be the dominant partner. Maybe I wanted to show that I'm the boss, I'm the strongest.'

Then Sisanda's need to dominate through violence became sexual.

BH: Did you ever rape [the women] to show you were dominant or have sex with them after you fought them?
SM: [Pause] Yes.
BH: Was this with your girlfriends?
SM: Ja.
BH: What would happen? You would kick them and then have sex with them?

SM: Ja. I would do that.
BH: Did it feel good?
SM: It made me feel better.
BH: Was it the sex that made you feel better or the control?
SM: Maybe it's the control. Maybe it was in the fact that it made me feel in control.

This was the dark shadow haunting Sisanda's nomadic wandering. Instead of the carefree lover leaving a trail of aching hearts and whispered endearments, there is the spectre of sudden violence, the heavy meaty thud of kicks landing on thigh or belly, rape as punishment for rejections that perhaps only Sisanda perceived: 'I must dominate to be the man. This is showing them who I am.'

He was never arrested for domestic violence or convicted of any of the assaults against his many girlfriends.

Sisanda talks very little about his wife and his one longer-term girlfriend, Amelia. They are shadows at the edge of the stage, separate from the main drama, although neither was safe from his violence. He talks more about the various women who rejected him. Perhaps his story has no space for women who may have played a more positive and supportive role. However, he speaks in depth about his eldest brother's second wife, Nandi, who now entered his story and wreaked havoc.

It started with his eldest brother's fall from grace. Sisanda's inner representation of his brother, the Elder Brother, was an image of one-dimensional perfection. Purely good and clever, and (as a pastor) even holy. The real person of his brother was more human, and more flawed: he had an affair, divorced his wife and married his mistress. She, Nandi, became Sisanda's nemesis.

Typically, Sisanda is reluctant to say anything directly negative about anyone associated with his beloved brother. As we talk, though, it's clear what he thinks of Nandi. He sees her as materialistic and grasping. Worse still, in a series of snippets and suggestions, Sisanda implies that Nandi looked down on him. She rejected him (maybe even sexually).

I imagine Nandi as confident and bold, the sort of woman who would enrage a man like Sisanda, who so desired dominance. He was helpless to do anything to her, though. Nandi was protected by the influence of the Elder Brother.

Sisanda blamed Nandi for his brother's downfall. His brother started to drink, Sisanda explains tersely, and then became ill. What Sisanda couldn't control in his external world affected his inner story. Suddenly, the Rejecting Woman took on the characteristics Sisanda gave Nandi: materialistic, selfish, arrogant, the reason for a good man's downfall.

Sisanda's eldest brother was evicted from church; then, as if completing his disgrace, he died.

> BH: How did it feel when he died?
> SM: I was angry. When my brother died, I was angry. I was angry with myself, I was angry with God, I was even angrier with his wife.

Just as he had felt when his parents died almost 20 years before, Sisanda was angry at God. The presence of his brother had always strengthened Sisanda's positive internal characters. With his brother's death, the Good Family Man's controlling influence collapsed.

Sisanda tried to become a pastor himself, perhaps to take his brother's place.

> BH: Did anyone get in the way of you becoming a minister?
> SM: The church constitution, the constitution of the church.

Sisanda says he 'didn't have a friend' to help support him in these efforts – 'it was just me alone'. He didn't have 'someone to stand by me, to fight for me. The church, they didn't take me seriously'.

> BH: So, you were angry with them?
> SM: I was angry with God. I wanted to leave the church.

The childhood rage at rejection, at the root of his characters, roared back into his life, a haunted echo from the past: 'I was angry at God.'

Shortly after the watershed year of 1994, Sisanda committed the first rape for which he was convicted. He talks about it reluctantly, in a quiet, hesitant voice. The story of this crime is a verbal fog: unclear, hesitant, jumbled.

Nomsa Mathetsa was the teenage daughter of someone with whom he'd had a secret affair. Sisanda says that he had previously 'proposed' to Nomsa (propositioned her) but had never had sex with her.

Nomsa heard from her mother that Sisanda was travelling to the nearby city in which he had a house, and asked him for a lift. He says that, on the trip, he was touching and kissing her. He says, 'She never said, "Don't touch".' Sisanda says that after they arrived, 'We went to the sea and then we ... I had sex with her.'

> BH: She said it was okay to have sex?
> SM: Mm ... Ja ... [Stammers] We had sex.

Sisanda ponders that perhaps she let him have sex with her because she feared him, or was worried about being stranded in the city. He does admit that later they had a 'big fight' when he 'forced' himself on her, slapping her twice, and she bit him. After this, Sisanda says, she slept over at his house but woke up early the next morning and took off without waking him.

Sisanda does not seem to see his sex with Nomsa as rape. Yet, as the police accounts spelt out, it was. The police account stated that when they arrived at the beach, Sisanda began to strangle Nomsa but she recovered. He then took her to a house, where he tried to rape her. When she resisted, he hit her. Then he did rape her. Nomsa escaped to a nearby home, telling the occupant what had happened to her.

Remember, Nomsa wasn't the first woman Sisanda had raped. He had admitted that he 'forced' sexual partners when they 'rejected' him by disagreeing with him or having other partners. The difference here was that Nomsa hadn't rejected him; she was merely associated with a former sexual partner of his. This foreshadows the horror of what was to come.

The life Sisanda had built started to fall apart. Aged only 30, he had committed rapes and his marriage was disintegrating.

Then he was diagnosed HIV-positive. This was years before

anti-retroviral treatments became widely available in South Africa, allowing HIV-positive people to live longer, healthier lives. In the late 1990s, an HIV-positive diagnosis in South Africa felt like, and often was, a death sentence. Foremost in Sisanda's mind, though, was the fear that his diagnosis would mean he could no longer work, robbing him of his role as the Good Family Man.

> It made me angry because, at home, I was the breadwinner with my two brothers and one sister. So I had to see that there was enough food on the table. So I was angry. I didn't want to accept it. I could not accept it. I had to be strong, not for myself, but for my family's sake.

He continues in a lower tone, with frequent pauses, saying that he wishes he could meet the person who gave him HIV, so he could take revenge himself.

To add to his stress, his wife's ex-husband approached her about access to their children and Sisanda 'feared he was going to take her away' from him: the fear of rejection had finally breached the walls of his family.

Previously, under the combined influence of the Good Family Man and the Elder Brother, Sisanda had managed to keep his family life separate from the activities of the Vengeful Lover. Now, the last of these divisions collapsed as the character of the Good Family Man faded from his narrative: Sisanda lashed out at his wife, hitting her.

His sister was worried enough about Sisanda's violence to make an appointment for him to see a psychologist. He never went.

For Sisanda, there were all sorts of different things going awry in his life, all at the same time, and during our interview it is evident that he is struggling to understand how and why it all went wrong.

> BH: Do you think if anything had happened differently that you wouldn't have committed these murders?
> SM: [Very quietly] Yes.

Sisanda had almost reached the dream of the Good Family Man, and now it was slipping through his fingers. Without the fulfilment offered by the Good Family Man, the darker release promised by the Vengeful Lover, in dynamic interaction with the Rejecting Woman, beckoned.

At this point, Sisanda's story gets even messier: not just gory, but confused too. The fog in which Nomsa's rape happened starts to spread.

Sisanda's seething anger was bubbling over. A woman no longer needed to reject him to be a victim of his violence. She could be a virtual stranger and still be raped.

Listening to Sisanda describe his crimes, a grim pattern emerges. When a woman didn't reject him directly, his story of these crimes is vague, confused and jumbled. He'll leave out details that appeared in the crime dockets or in the media. In sharp contrast, when Sisanda felt a woman had rejected him, his story is precise. He is clear and decisive. He was also more violent, more lethal: the more closely a woman was associated with the Rejecting Woman character in his internal story, the more likely she was to die.

The three murders Sisanda was convicted of occurred in the same year he was diagnosed with HIV. He was also charged with two counts of rape (one of which related to the offence against Nomsa Mathetsa) and one of attempted rape.

Sisanda denies he tried to rape Paulina Mbuli, a 28-year-old schoolteacher whom he had agreed to give a lift to, to a neighbouring town. Police accounts stated they were travelling at night. Just before they reached their destination, Sisanda stopped the car at the roadside, grabbed Paulina and throttled her until she became weak. He tried to remove her clothes, but she fought back violently. Sisanda responded angrily, and in the ensuing struggle Paulina fell from the vehicle.

There are obvious parallels between this offence and the rape of Nomsa a year earlier: both victims had sought a lift with him, both attacks had occurred at the roadside en route, and both victims had elicited an angry reaction from Sisanda and had been throttled when they resisted.

Sisanda drove off with Paulina's suitcase containing her clothes. Paulina walked into town and laid a charge.

When we discuss this offence, Sisanda looks away, repeats his denials, then looks down. I am not sure whether this is a sign of dishonesty or simply due to his awkwardness around the topic.

Four days after the attack on Paulina, Sisanda bumped into a recent ex-girlfriend of his, the young police officer Stella Mogotsi. Stella was a friend of his brother's second wife, Nandi. He says he wanted to ask Stella why she stopped their relationship and began ignoring him: 'Was it because I had nothing or was it because [of] what Nandi said to her?'

Stella told him that Nandi thought he wasn't good enough for her.

> SM: Stella said it, so that made me angry afterwards.
> Because the friendship with Nandi was going down.
> It was back to where we started; we were splitting up
> again. She was starting to make enemies for me. That
> is how I look at it, you see.
> BH: So Nandi was starting to make you enemies?
> SM: Yes... I was angry. Very angry.

Sisanda's reaction was predictable.

> Nandi made me angry, and Stella made me angry. But I
> didn't want to kill Stella, but I wanted to hurt Stella. I wanted
> her to know that she hurt me. So I got to hurt her ... She
> was talking so boldly; she was so sure of herself. Only
> because she had that gun with her.

Stella, as a police member, was carrying her service pistol, a Z-88.

> Maybe the gun made her bold, the gun made her strong.
> But when I took the gun away from her, she was no longer
> that strong, self-assured person.

He says he is 'afraid' of guns, doesn't like guns, but he took it anyway, and later gave it to Nandi for safekeeping.

Unlike with the rapes, Sisanda narrates the murder of Stella fluently and with certainty. He didn't talk much to her, swiftly binding her hands behind her back. 'I never shouted at her. I said I was angry, and I said the things that made me angry.' He then strangled Stella with wire. According to him, he didn't rape her. He admits that while he never intended to kill her, 'what I did killed her.'

It appears that either during the struggle or after she was dead, Stella's hands were freed and the wire around her neck was attached to her belt. Sisanda then drove on for a distance and dumped her body near a bus stop.

> BH: How did you feel when you were tying her up?
> SM: I have to say I was angry.
> BH: And just after, when you dropped her off at the roadside?
> SM: Relieved. I can say maybe I was relieved I got rid of her.
> BH: Relieved to have stopped her talking?
> SM: Ja.

When I ask him if the pistol reminded him of Stella, he says emphatically, 'Yes. That's why I immediately got rid of the gun, gave it to someone else.'

> BH: Did it make you feel bad?
> SM: It made me sad. Not bad, as such, but sad. Sometimes you do something that you cannot use. There's this guy who sings a song, 'If I could turn back the hand of time' ...
> BH: Is that how you felt about Stella?
> SM: Ja.

Saying this, Sisanda breaks down in tears.

Sisanda then says that just after arriving in prison, he felt like he was going mad, tormented by 'many things on my mind'.

> I remember, with Stella, I have never seen something like that – a person that's dying, instead of asking God to help her, she said, 'God, please forgive Sisanda.' I will never forget. Even today, I won't.

As we spoke his narrative returned, many times, to Stella, a victim of whom he cannot free his mind.

Nandi had long nettled Sisanda. With the killing of Stella, he directly implicated her in a murder: he blamed her for turning Stella against him and gave her Stella's gun. Both Stella's rejection of

Sisanda and her association with Nandi contributed to her death.

In this event, we see his inner characters change: the Vengeful Lover was now provoked more easily, to greater violence. The dynamic between characters changed, too. Previously, the Rejecting Woman character only goaded the Vengeful Lover by rejecting Sisanda; now, the Rejecting Woman was blamed for poisoning Sisanda's relationships with others. Sisanda could now target someone who was associated with his preferred victim. Chillingly, it hints that the Vengeful Lover, acting through Sisanda, might claim a substitute victim if his preferred target wasn't available.

At this point, a few months after Stella's death, Portia Mashabela entered the story.

Sisanda was struggling financially, living a semi-nomadic life, constantly on the move across the Eastern Cape, between jobs, his wife and his girlfriends. For whatever reason, he rented a room in a house Nandi owned in a large town. It was a big four-bedroom house with a garage and servants' quarters out the back. Nandi also lived there, renting out the other rooms. One of the other tenants was 26-year-old Portia, a colleague of Nandi's.

When asked to narrate what happened with Portia, Sisanda's first response is ominous: 'Things were not going well between me and Nandi.' He mentions, in an almost inaudible voice, that he had 'proposed to' Nandi and that she had turned him down. It is not clear what his intention was – sex or marriage or a relationship – and he does not refer to it again. But he implies that this rejection from Nandi affected Portia's attitude towards him.

In a fast, low voice – angry just talking about it – Sisanda says:

One day, Portia started to have a [pauses] negative attitude towards me. She would joke about my car, my old car. She would say that I was not giving a good impression to the house because members of the public would come there and see my car. She would say such jokes. I would laugh but inside I was not laughing.

He goes on to narrate an incident where he, because he 'like(s) to play physically', playfully tripped Portia and caught her before she fell. Portia did not take this well and retaliated.

> She said that if you tore my valuables, you won't be able to pay for that because the money you're working [for] won't be able to pay for these items. Ei! She was making me angry. I wanted to slap her, but something said to me, 'No, don't.'

His voice not slowing, Sisanda says that after this incident he told Nandi that he would be moving out because of his clashes with Portia. He left the house and went to live with a girlfriend nearby. Later, he returned to Nandi's house to collect his remaining possessions and found the locks had been changed.

Provoked to rage, he phoned Nandi, asking why people were 'making funny tricks'. Nandi dismissed him, saying he must take his things and get out of the house. Sisanda waited outside. When the women arrived,

> They were driving this latest BMW, this E class. They parked the car in the driveway. Portia went into the house. I said to Portia, 'Don't lock the house,' because I wanted to get my things out of there. Portia walked into the house with the key. She came back and locked the house, then got into the car and drove away.

It appears that the women's flaunting their wealth angered Sisanda almost as much as their ignoring him. In Sisanda's story, Portia shared the materialist character he had previously associated with Nandi.

Sisanda wasn't able to return until two days later, and in the interim 'I had to do without changing my clothes'.

He arrived at half past seven in the evening. Nandi, who Sisanda refers to in this part of his story as 'my sister', was not there. Portia gave Sisanda a hostile reception:

> She asked me, 'Eh [sneering], what do [you] want?' I said, 'I have come to fetch my things.' She was looking behind me, swearing, telling me my sister told me she doesn't want me there any more. I asked her, 'Am I going to get my things?' She said, 'No, you must get out of here. You must come when your sister is here.'

Rudely and repeatedly dismissed and insulted by a woman he found desirable, someone associated with Nandi, the rejecter, Sisanda was more provoked than he could bear.

In his haste to tell this part of his story, Sisanda's words come out in a jumble.

> That made me angry. There are three steps in the house, down steps. I kicked her. She fell down [the steps], then I put my knee on her, when she fell there. Then I proceeded to choke her. She had pantyhose in her hand, and I pulled the pantyhose up, then I pressed with my knee in the back of her. I was telling her all the things that she said that made me angry, all of them. After about five minutes I let her go. I thought, 'Okay, I have killed.'

As with Stella, he had strangled Portia with a ligature, while telling her how she had brought this on herself.

'Funny,' Sisanda sighs, as if sitting back, satisfied. His speech slows and becomes measured and clear.

> SM: To tell you the truth, I didn't feel sad. [Pauses] I didn't feel sad. I was not worried.
> BH: So, you felt angry while you were doing it. Then, afterwards?
> SM: I was not sad, as such, or worried that I had killed someone, you see. Maybe inside of me there was a thing that said, 'You've revenged. She did you wrong. You took your revenge. You see, what you did maybe is right, you see.' Maybe that's how I felt, but to tell you the truth, I was not sad. [Pauses] You see, in Portia's case, I was not angry with myself after that one. I can … I can say I sort of felt relieved, as if I have solved the most difficult problem I ever had.

Later, I ask him whether killing Portia was enjoyable.

> SM: I don't think 'enjoying' it is the right word. I revenged.
> BH: It was necessary?
> SM: Ja.

The offence that most obviously matched the relationships between his internal characters, the Rejecting Woman and Vengeful Lover, was the most satisfying.

Again, Sisanda had committed murder impulsively. He says he didn't rape Portia, and he left her fully clothed. 'I told myself now, "Ei, I have killed someone," so I took her to the garage, put mats over her, then thought what to do.' He left her body hidden there for a week.

> BH: She just lay there? No one knew what had happened
>   to her?
> SM: [Very quietly] Ja.

After a week, Sisanda returned, retrieved Portia's corpse and loaded it into his car. He drove to a settlement about 50 kilometres away, with an unknowing girlfriend in the car. He says it didn't matter to him where he left the body; he just wanted to be rid of it.

Portia's body was found wrapped in a floral sheet and a plastic bag from Nandi's garage. The stockings she was strangled with were still tied tightly around her neck.

While Sisanda's behaviour at the crime scene seems clear, his behaviour after the offence was not. As with Stella, Sisanda stole an item from Portia: her cellphone. Again, he can't explain why he committed this theft.

This offence shows what happened to Sisanda's story when a victim was associated with the inner character of the Rejecting Woman. His description is clear and precise, and his revenge deadly and focused. He can explain the reasons behind his actions, too. Outside the direct influence of this character, however, Sisanda struggles to explain why he did things, such as why he stole something or even why he killed. This is nowhere better illustrated than in his final, and in many ways most horrifying, murder.

Throughout his trial, Sisanda denied killing his stepdaughter, 15-year-old Zondi, a child of his wife's first marriage. (Zondi, Sisanda says, looked like her mother.)

By this point, Sisanda's own marriage to Thembeni was falling apart. He had already reacted violently to the suggestion that Thembeni's first husband be allowed access to their children, of whom Zondi was one. Now, Thembeni was planning to divorce him.

Sisanda admits he was the cause of the breakup of his marriage.

SM: I was the cause of the divorce.
BH: Because of things you were doing?
SM: Yes. Because of things, like ...

At this point Sisanda is overcome by emotion and falls silent, crying. Perhaps, confronted with the part he played in thwarting the dreams embodied in the Good Family Man, he is overcome with loss and regret. Maybe it is the story to come that makes him weep.

He continues, and the story of Zondi's murder is punctuated by pauses.

Just under a month after Portia's death, Sisanda went to stay with his wife at her house, as he normally did over school holidays. Zondi was there visiting his wife, her mother.

He woke up early that Sunday morning, only to find that Thembeni had left.

SM: She wrote me a letter telling me that she doesn't want to see me again. And she also sent back the watch I gave her for our fourth anniversary. Then I said, 'Ish, she is serious ...' I had to get her, I had to get hold of her, but there was no way, she didn't want to see me again.
BH: Did you want her back, or were you just angry at her?
SM: I wanted her back. I wanted her back.

Sisanda phoned his wife, asking her to come home and speak with him. She refused, saying she would be spending that night at a friend's.

He went to where his wife was staying but the friend wouldn't allow him in.

Sisanda intended to find his wife, kill her, and then commit suicide.

Just to finish it off there and then. I was going to shoot Thembeni and then I was going to shoot myself.

He tried to find the firearm his sister owned but couldn't. He then returned to the house he shared with Thembeni to wash. There, he made plans to retrieve Stella's Z-88 from Nandi to fulfil his murder–suicide plans.

Speaking slowly and deliberately, pausing often and sighing, he says,

> Zondi [was] at the wrong place, at the wrong time. Because that day, I wanted to hurt her mother. But unfortunately, I couldn't get my hands on her mother. So, I took what I knew she really loved, her daughter. I knew Thembeni loved Zondi. I knew that Zondi's father loved Zondi as well, very much, you see. Now, I told myself, this is the time to get even.

As before, the decision to murder was taken impulsively. However, rather than immediately attack his victim, Sisanda decided to lure her away.

Sisanda followed Zondi as she walked to the nearby taxi rank, planning to catch the same taxi she did. A brown Volkswagen Kombi arrived and Zondi got on. There was a spare seat for Sisanda.

When the taxi arrived at the square where passengers were disgorged, Sisanda told Zondi, 'Listen, there is something I want you to give to a church elder from our church, so can you please come with me and fetch this thing in my flat?'

Zondi didn't want to be late for Sunday school, so asked if they could hurry. Sisanda took her to the bar below a flat he owned. He bought a quarter of gin and two Cokes, one of which he gave to Zondi.

> SM: Then I poured the quarter of gin into the Coke and then I drank it.
>
> BH: What did you do that for?
>
> SM: I'm sure I was taking some strength for what I was going to do. I was taking the shyness out of me. I was trying to get rid of the fright, of being frightened. Because I told myself I had to do this. I was going to pay Thembeni back where it hurt most.

Then 'everything happened suddenly', he says. Sounding ashamed, in a clear, slow voice, he says:

71

> So after maybe three, five minutes, I took Zondi. 'Come
> here, there is something up in the flat.' I strangled her. I
> raped her first. I won't lie, you see.

According to police reports, he strangled Zondi with a nylon rope,
which he tied to the leg of a chair before he left.

Leaving Zondi where she had died, he locked the door of the
flat and went home.

> SM: But I couldn't sleep that night.
> BH: What was going through your head?
> SM: I was afraid. I was thinking about what I have caused,
> what have I done. How am I going to forgive myself?
> Because even now, even today, [pause] there are
> certain things that I can forgive and forget, but not
> Zondi. I regret Zondi.

I ask Sisanda whether he felt that he had 'revenged', as he did after
Portia.

He pauses, then replies, 'I felt sorrow. For myself and for Zondi.'
He repeats that, in Zondi's case, 'I won't be able to forgive myself,
or to forget ...'

In his final murder, Sisanda's internal characters seemed to
have played a terrible trick on him. The Vengeful Lover had always
whispered in his ear that revenge was the only course of action
when wronged, the only way to make himself feel better. The
Rejecting Woman character in his narrative encouraged revenge
and deserved violence. Together, these characters beguiled Sisanda
into the belief that this next step in revenge was justified. In doing
so, they laid a brutal psychological trap for him.

Once he had murdered Zondi, the realisation hit him; this
wasn't the hot-headed passion and revenge that, to Sisanda, made
the murders of Stella and Portia seem justified. Instead, his actions
seemed to have had a cold malice and he was confronted by their
fundamental cruelty. He had been lied to by his own story.

Even worse, this offence broke the separation he had always
tried to keep between the positive and negative characters in his
inner story. Maybe this is why Sisanda denied Zondi's murder for

so long: he couldn't reconcile what he had done with the story he told himself, and so he shut it out.

In Sisanda's narrative, this offence was followed almost immediately by his arrest. In reality, he was on the run for more than a month.

Let's end Sisanda's story as we started it. This time, let's zoom out, not over the external landscape of the Eastern Cape, but over the internal landscape of Sisanda's story.

> BH: You said you're not a serial killer. What would you describe yourself as?
> SM: [Laughs] I don't know. [Laughs again] Really, I don't know. But I'm not one. Because I didn't go around killing people without a reason, or enjoying killing people.
> BH: You say if you're a serial killer, you would have done it for no reason or you would have liked doing it?
> SM: Ja ...
> BH: Whenever you killed someone, you had a reason?
> SM: Yes.

This perfectly distils the role of Sisanda's characters. Sisanda's anger seems to have been life-long. Perhaps he was destined to be a violent man, but the characters in his story gave him a reason to kill. Without the destructive dynamic between his characters, it's difficult to imagine him murdering repeatedly. Look how he describes a crime against someone who embodied the Rejecting Woman, like Portia or Stella. The descriptions are clear, and he uses terms like 'solved a problem' or 'a relief'. Contrast this with his description of his final crime, first denying, then weeping in regret.

Think now of all the characters in Sisanda's story on a movie set together. The action starts with the vivid violence, the constant battle between the Lonely Child and the world. The most complex character is the one associated with his violence, loneliness and frustration. The Lonely Child then becomes the Vengeful Lover. Unlike the Lonely Child, though, the Vengeful Lover doesn't just lash out at everyone, instead focusing his anger on the Rejecting Woman.

This battle takes centre stage in Sisanda's story, and all the attention is on it. These characters hog the spotlight, while the characters associated with other people, or with other parts of Sisanda's character, get pushed into the shadows at the edge of the stage. This, then, transforms his actions in the real world.

This is the third killer story: revenge, and specifically revenge against a victim who, in the murderer's story, deserves it. The revenge story justifies violence and removes any other option.

4 Michael: Disintegration

The crimes

It is sometimes the case with serial murderers that those hunting them are not aware of their serial nature until arrests are made. In several cases, it has been one offence that has led to the arrest, and then the offender himself will admit to many more murders. This is one such instance.

On the eve of the dawning of the new South Africa in the 1990s, the body of a homeless child called Sam was found at a primary school. The child had been sodomised and strangled to death, and his murder would remain unsolved for several years. Although this crime would be linked to the offender, he was ultimately not convicted of it. Many suspected, however, this was the first crime in his series.

One of the main reasons that this offender's crimes would go unlinked for so long was that he veered quite significantly outside of the 'normal' victim profile selection we often see with serial offenders. Between his first known murder and his second, he significantly changed both the gender and the age group of the victim.

It's worth noting, though, that victim profile is not always limited to obvious external specifics such as age, gender, race and other superficial qualities. Sometimes, the offender will target a far wider group, such as those who are vulnerable due to their homeless status, by virtue of the work they do – sex workers, for instance – or people living with substance-use disorders, or even unemployed people who are desperate for work. This can make linking crimes to one another very difficult and, whether done knowingly or not, it certainly works in the offender's favour in staying undetected for longer.

Today, with DNA advances, linking crimes with a sexual element, where bodily fluids from the offender may be present, is much easier. Victim-profile linking therefore becomes slightly less important if the law-enforcement agency in question is able to access a database of crimes into which DNA profiles from unsolved cases have been entered. The series in question here, though, occurred during a time when DNA testing was not as prevalently used as it is today in South Africa, and we also did not have a database available for unsolved cases. So when the offender suddenly started killing adult females, the police would not automatically have believed the child murders to be linked to these. The victimology was so different, a serial killer would not have been immediately suspected.

The second victim in this series was killed eight months after the first. The victim, an adult female named Maria Stolz, was found strangled to death. Maria was known to be a sex worker in the area, and an autopsy showed that she had engaged in vaginal sex before her death, but there were indications that anal rape had occurred that had probably coincided with her death. She had been strangled with a piece of her own clothing.

Sadly, it is not uncommon for sex workers to be murdered by their clients. According to a report by the Sex Workers Education & Advocacy Taskforce (Sweat), in 2019 homicide was the predominant cause of death among women working in the sex trade, and things were certainly no different in 1990s. Solving such murders is difficult because the perpetrator is often a stranger to the victim.

Although it would be identified only in retrospect, each of the murders in this series was showing a progression for the offender. In Maria's murder, he had for the first time experienced an intense rush from strangling the victim while he raped her; he would later describe it as the most intense climax he'd ever had. Perhaps because of this, his next victim would also be a sex worker.

Six months after Maria's body was found, the body of Millicent Smit was discovered in a park near a hotel where she was known to solicit clients for sex work. This autopsy would find that the victim had been raped after death. The offender would later confirm that this was his first experience of necrophilia – sex with a deceased person – and it would mark the start of new behaviour for the killer.

Another tragic common feature in serial murders in South Africa, especially when vulnerable victims are targeted, is that many of the victims remain unidentified. When there is no family to open a missing person's report and sometimes even no record of the person on the Department of Home Affairs system (in the case of homeless children), identification is almost impossible. In the case of sex workers, they will often not have anyone looking for them, due to the transient nature of their work, but often these women will be identified through arrestee databases if they'd been detained for solicitation or related offences in the past.

At this point in the series, the offender switched back to his original victim profile – street children. Both of the victims who followed Millicent would remain unidentified; deceased persons who were not claimed within 30 days were buried by the state often in unmarked graves.

The first unidentified male child victim was about 14 years old. The offender raped and strangled him and then hid his body in bushes. The child's body would remain there for two years, and when the offender eventually pointed it out to police after his arrest, he confirmed that he had returned to the body on several occasions to rape the deceased.

From this point onward, the killer would go to far more trouble to conceal the bodies of his victims. He also began to insert newspaper into their bodily orifices to prevent insect infestation so that he could perform necrophilic acts on the bodies for longer.

The second unidentified child victim was also about 14, and was also hidden in bushes, but he was killed at a historical site, so visitors there picked up on the odour of decomposition and he was found relatively quickly.

After these two victims, there was a very large gap in the series. In piecing the puzzle together later, it would be determined that the offender had been in a psychiatric facility for about 30 days due to domestic-violence issues and accusations of child abuse, although this accounted for only a very small portion of what would eventually be an almost four-year gap between victims. It is far more likely that there were other victims during this period who have never been linked to the perpetrator. After all, the police would eventually rely on the offender himself to identify many of his crimes, so if he didn't share all of them, it's likely no one would ever know.

The next murder for which this offender would be convicted occurred four years later, and it presented yet another progression in his pattern of behaviour. When the body of Ntombi Nkosi was found, she had been anally raped and strangled, but she had also been horrifically mutilated with a knife. The offender had inserted a knife into her vagina and cut open her pubic area. He had then sliced off her nipples; they were missing from the scene. It would later emerge that the killer had cannibalised them.

In comparing the various scenes post-arrest, the police would note that at some point the offender had started to strip his victims naked and remove their clothing from the scene. It transpired that he loitered at his murder scenes, watching the way the police processed them, seeing what they looked for and did; he noticed that they paid special attention to any evidence that may have clung to the victims' clothing, which is why he started stripping them down.

The progression to mutilation and cannibalism is interesting from a criminological perspective for two reasons. If the offender had indeed not committed any other murders in the large time gap, this offence could have represented an explosion of pent-up rage and frustration. It could, however, reinforce the possibility that there were other victims during this time period that were either never found or just not linked to the offender. Perhaps this apparent escalation was less of a progression and more of a continuation. Either way, the killer was to make a crucial error which would eventually bring his reign of terror to an end and reveal his horrendous crimes to the world.

Two months after the brutal murder of Ntombi Nkosi, 10-year-old Melissa Joubert disappeared from outside her home. The girl was last spotted speaking to her biological father, Michael Joubert, who did not live with the family. Joubert was known to the local Child Protection Unit of the SAPS, as previous partners had made allegations of child abuse against him.

Joubert was called in and interviewed. He claimed that he had no idea where his daughter was, and that he had left her sitting on the pavement outside the house after speaking to her briefly that day.

While the police continued to search for the missing 10-year-old, the body of another sex worker was discovered. Liesel Robbins had been raped and strangled to death. A plastic bag had been inserted into her throat, and her body had been dumped beside a wall on which the killer had scrawled a message: 'People should not steal.'

The body of another unidentified, homeless child was discovered at the same primary school where the body of Michael's first victim, Sam, had been found. Although Joubert wasn't convicted of Sam's death, he was convicted of the murder of this unknown child, found in the same place and killed in the same way as Sam had been two years before.

By the beginning of 1997, three years after the body of the first victim was discovered, Melissa Joubert was still missing, and police seemed no closer to finding her than on the day she'd last been seen. The prime suspect in her disappearance, her father Michael, had, however, just come back onto the police radar. The woman Joubert was living with at the time had reported him for allegedly anally raping her two young sons. It does not appear that immediate action was taken to arrest Joubert, and as soon as he heard that a case had been opened against him, he fled. The police's delay in acting would have deadly consequences for one more child.

Not long after Michael Joubert moved areas to escape police scrutiny, 12-year-old Bobby Whitehead disappeared while walking near his home. For the next 24 hours or so, his mother assumed he was with his grandmother, who lived nearby. When Bobby's mother called his grandmother to find out when he would be home, she discovered that her son was not there and immediately reported him missing.

The same Child Protection Unit officers who were investigating the now-cold missing person's case of Melissa Joubert arrived at the Whitehead home to begin their investigation into Bobby's disappearance. One of their first tasks was to interview all of Bobby's young friends as, so often, this is a vital source of information. One young boy had indeed made a crucial sighting: he had last seen Bobby walking away from his home with an older man. He didn't know the man's real name, but he knew Bobby's family knew him well – the boy said the man had briefly lived with the Whiteheads, and Bobby had called him 'Takkies' – which is why he didn't think much about seeing them together.

The nickname, known to the officers, belonged to the suspect in Melissa Joubert's disappearance, as well as the rape of two young boys: Michael Joubert.

Joubert was questioned about Bobby's disappearance and he denied any involvement. He provided an alibi for the time period in question and was released. When that alibi did not check out, however, he was arrested.

In the days that followed, a detective trained in serial-offender behaviour as well as psychologically motivated crimes interviewed Joubert.

When a serial murderer kills and there is no DNA, no behavioural similarities or even (hauntingly) no police reports of a missing child, how are the crimes linked to one another? They aren't. Or rather, they weren't in the mid-1990s when Joubert was offending. At that time, a good investigator followed up leads and, at the crucial moment in an interview, pushed harder at the suspect. In the case of Joubert, it was the investigator's educated hunch about the man sitting in front of him that made all the difference.

The investigator trusted and went with his hunch, used his skill and training, and Joubert confessed to the rape and murder of Bobby Whitehead. He also admitted that he had murdered his daughter, Melissa. He claimed that the child was being molested by her stepfather and he had killed her to save her.

Joubert would take investigators to a site where he had been living rough and it was there that they found Melissa's skeletonised remains. Joubert had been sleeping beside his daughter's dead body for months.

Joubert went on to admit to several other murders and police pulled the dockets for these cases as he provided details that helped them identify which murders he was referring to. There were occasions where Joubert provided details about murders that the police could not find. It is still unknown whether these murders actually happened and the dockets were lost, or if Joubert simply got them confused with existing cases. Some of the victims had been decomposing in bushes for a long time when they were recovered; it's unlikely they ever would have been found had Joubert not pointed them out.

Michael Joubert was found guilty of seven murders. He was handed down several life sentences, and he cried as he heard his fate.

Michael's killer story

I keep sneaking glances at Michael's hands. They aren't the hands I had expected. I'd anticipated big hands, calloused by a life of manual work – strangler's hands – but they're small, almost delicate. When we shake hands, they aren't rough or hard.

The hands curled on the desk next to my questionnaire papers and tape recorder do not look like strangler's hands. I've seen what they can do, though, in the photos of the women and children in fields or under highway flyovers, sprawled in the vulnerability of death, their faces showing signs, in bruised eyelids and swollen tongues, of the last awful relentless pressure of those hands.

To be fair, Micheal himself looks ominous. Thickset and stocky as a rugby prop, he walks with his arms held away from his body and his head low, almost hunched, an effect accentuated by a thick neck and shoulders. The first impression is that he's glowering from beneath his dark, heavy brows; beneath a dark receding hairline, very dark brown eyes staring out over a black beard. A tattoo of a woman decorates his forearm.

This formidable appearance is contradicted by his rather quiet, polite demeanour when we first start speaking. His beard and hair are short and well groomed. He apologises for the bad fit of his clothes, saying that the prison doesn't have anything for someone of his size.

The arresting detective had said Michael was a 'neat freak', laughingly describing how they had shared burgers and Michael had scolded the detective when he spilled on himself, angrily calling him a 'pig' and saying 'eat properly like a person'. His stepmother reported that Michael had been the same as a boy: refusing to eat his food if it got mixed up on his plate, peas touching rice or tomato sauce nudging an egg yolk.

Michael is the only serial murderer I met three times: once as part of another research project, again on an informal visit with the investigating officer, and the third time to record this interview. So when we speak, he dives right in at the deep end. 'Do you want to know why I did it?' he asks me, immediately.

He can be funny, and likeable, and his story is peppered with unusual words or unexpected turns of phrase, hooking my attention. His tone rises and falls, in turns casually indifferent, thrumming with vague threat, and rising with the focused intensity of an evangelical preacher. The last happens especially when describing the abuse of children, or his own abuse. I jot in my notes that at these times, 'His eyes become half closed, hooded, a blank, lazy, dangerous face.'

He speaks with his hands: when describing a murder, saying 'you feel ten times bigger than usual, you feel great like a giant', he makes the motions of bulging muscles in the air over his arms and shoulders. Talking about taking children, his hands sweep, as if showing a child snatched away by the wind.

Michael's world is claustrophobic. After I speak with him for the first time, I come back late to my student accommodation and draw strange pictures to rid my head of the images planted there – the sense that a trapdoor has opened into another world, existing cheek by jowl with normality. A contributor to that strange sense of discombobulation is Michael's vulnerability. Alongside the terror of crime scenes and murder is a deep sense of vulnerability. Unexpectedly, as we talk, his face becomes that of a child lost in a cruel world.

Michael opens his story like a monster from a fairytale, a beast who listens and watches for parents who mistreat their children, then spirits the child away as punishment.

> MJ: I'll see kids being abused. I will tell you not to, and you tell me to go away. Later, you will look for your child. You won't find them.
>
> BH: You'll take them away?
>
> MJ: Yes. [Angrily, slurred, with malice] I'll come and listen to your crying and your false pain over your child, and I'll laugh inside. I take children to peace. I always said you mustn't abuse a child because then I will take the child. Then I will hear, I want God to hear, how that child screams when the child is taken. Then [gentler tone] that's how it went. I would take them away, to a place; then have these verwissellings [permutations].

A 'permutation' refers to a different way of arranging things, changing their order, transforming them. When Michael transformed, he would release the children from the pain they had suffered. He did this by murdering them in his secret hideaways. Like a creature from a horror story, he kept the young bodies in his lair as souvenirs.

The very moment he's painted himself in terms of mythical horror, his story leaps to an anecdote of his own terrible abuse. Michael's story does this again and again: switching seamlessly between anecdotes of his murders and his own abuse. Hearing him speak, it's as if the abused child he used to be has leapt a three-decade gap, revenging himself in an instant.

Michael seemed cursed from the start. Born about 30 years before we spoke, in one of the working towns strung along the industrial spine of South Africa, he was promptly abandoned at a roadside, along with his elder sister. They were found by a domestic worker, who took them to her employer. According to the records, this person treated Michael terribly. A local family took pity on the apparently lice-infected and cigarette-burnt young child and took him in, along with his sister. This act of charity reportedly got them additional welfare grants, and Michael was the youngest of his foster brothers and sisters.

His biological mother returned to reclaim his sister, but not Michael.

Michael's narration of his life returns repeatedly to his time with his foster family. In particular, he says his stepmother would treat him differently from the other kids, and this 'scratched at me'. Lamenting that she never once 'said to me "my child", [never] just put her arm around me and took me aside and said, "my child"', he says his siblings were allowed to play and were showered with affection, while he was made to work. Angrily and passionately, he says,

> I never hear her say, 'I love you.' It's all just, 'Go do this, go do this,' when the other children are happily fooling about while I do garden work ... [I] don't know if my stepmom loved me, I didn't know.

Using one of his vivid images, he says, 'You can't give one child cake and give the other one bread to eat. Everything must be just like so.' He makes the motion of ordering things into neat piles, talking with his hands. 'They unsettled me terribly.'

> BH: Did you ever feel lonely?
> MJ: Definitely. Definitely.

I ask him when he first started to think about murder.

> I had a rage. I couldn't trust people. I was always hit. It makes your heart sore. It hurt me, it really hurt me. I couldn't talk about it. I was always wrong. There was no one I could

go to. It was pain, rage. It wasn't good. What's life worth for you if you're not trusted? What's life worth if you're a kid and you're attacked and abused, you don't get love?

He repeats these words again and again, a drumbeat to which his story dances, that of a wounded and cursed child alone in an unfriendly world. The Wounded Child was the first character in his story, and a ghost that haunted it throughout.

Michael was raped when he was five or six years old by a house father at his school hostel. His voice swells with passionate intensity, as it always does when describing his abuse.

> I was in a single room and I cried out, I screamed, 'God help me!' But nothing came; God didn't help me. I went to a psychologist to try to get help but they squashed it. They didn't believe me, and there was the same pain, the same pain I grew up with, of being not trusted and not believed. I carried a great pain around in me, a great heartbreak for many years. Every time I see a child getting raped, I have that. I have that pain because I know what it feels like to go through it.

This moment birthed the character of the Monster, which Michael eventually became.

Michael says he never went to church after that betrayal, when God didn't help him when called on. Talking about this as a 'grudge', Michael angrily lists his young self's questions for God.

> God, why did you throw me away? Why did you split me from my parents? Got, why was I brought up like this? God, what aim did you have for me?

Michael found out, aged between 10 and 12, that he had been abandoned as a child.

> I couldn't concentrate at school. I was told I was a weeskind [orphan] and I thought they said beeskind [beast child]. I went home and asked my mother what 'weeskind' was.

Perhaps worse of all for him, he says he was told that his biological mother had 'thrown him away'. This sense of being unwanted and outcast was a curse on the young Michael. When we first spoke, he had never met his biological mother. He wondered if maybe, had she taken him back, things would have been different, and some of his 'psychopathic traits', as he called them, may not have developed.

The one-letter difference between 'orphan' and 'beast child' foreshadowed the deeper split to come in Michael's internal characters. At some point, Michael became known by a nickname: Takkies. Presumably it had been bestowed on him by his family, as a cute moniker. When reporting conversations with his family, he always says that's what they called him. As his story unfolds, though, Takkies takes on sinister overtones as the name becomes increasingly associated with the internal character of the Monster.

Michael's stepmother corroborates his story of an unhappy schooling, misbehaving, being bullied by other children and liable to explode in sudden outbursts of angry violence. She says Michael was compulsively neat, and masturbated frequently from the age of ten, with other boys. Sexually precocious behaviour can be, as in his case, a sign of a child who has been sexually abused.

Michael doesn't describe his teenage years with the repetitive intensity of his younger days. Though he struggled to make progress at school, running away repeatedly, he eventually settled and achieved his Grade 11. He was then conscripted into the army, like all white boys his age in that era.

A suicide attempt cut his service short, and Michael followed his foster family to one of the country's coastal cities. There, he found unskilled and semi-skilled work, first in a factory, where he injured himself, then as a security guard, then finally as a fisherman, before seemingly drifting into unemployment. Michael enjoyed being at sea, away from the tumult of his life on land.

Michael met his first wife, Sarie, a short time before his twentieth birthday. They dated and later married, reportedly when the state welfare services threatened to remove their first child from their care. The marriage was an unhappy one, characterised by continual conflict and accusations of infidelity. Michael was admitted to a psychiatric hospital for a short period, given medication to keep him calm, then discharged back into the unhappy melee of his home life.

Michael's narrative gets unclear and confused when he discusses Sarie. Events jumble together and anecdotes are half-told then cut off as he jumps to another point in his timeline. I can't say why this may be. It could be that the vengeful tit-for-tat of his marriage does not fit the simple 'I am an innocent victim' narrative of his childhood. What comes through with utter clarity is the lasting hatred the relationship kindled. If his childhood rape birthed the character of the Monster, his relationship with Sarie brought it to maturity.

His narrative of his marriage is a string of anecdotes of mistrust and betrayal: him tricking Sarie by faking love letters from other men, and accusing her of infidelity; Sarie reporting him to the police or social services for various crimes. 'I can't talk about my first wife without bile in my throat,' he says. 'The pain!'

In later interviews with the police and media, Sarie mentioned Michael's high sex drive and predilection for rough sex. She reported Michael for assault three or four times, leading to short prison stays. Says Michael: 'It makes you tired. You can't go home. I couldn't see my kid in case she called the police.'

We segue into another anecdote of his being unheard and ignored at a court case for the custody of one of their children: 'If I ask for help, they ignore me, [but] if a woman goes there, they listen to the bitch.'

He accuses his wife repeatedly, throughout our interview, of being a prostitute and of spending the money he gave her to look after their children. While there is no unequivocal evidence to support these claims, both court documents and media reports suggest she was a woman struggling with her own demons of addiction and bad companions.

> I can't trust people, any people. I lost it because of my first wife. [Loudly, passionately] She is the reason I hate all whores. She didn't take care of the house. She whored. She gave me the pain of her being a whore and that's how I got a grudge against whores. If I saw a woman in the street asking me for sex, then I show her. Then I say, 'Come with me.'

The monster that had been seething in him had found what it

deemed a deserving victim. Michael picked Maria Stolz up on the road and murdered her at a nearby school.

> We go to a place, and I had sex with her. While I am on top of her, I [see] this jagged transformation. She changes into a monster-like dragon thing ...

Describing how he killed Maria while he was raping her, Michael says how sexually pleasurable the experience was and how intense his orgasm was. The curt brutality of his words echoes his actions; in his mind, sex and murder are inextricably linked, one leading to the other.

This story flows seamlessly back to a description of his hate for his wife, then to his being abandoned by his mother ('Why did they throw me away? Why didn't they come when I said, "Heaven help me"?') The Monster's revenge was linked back to the woman he blamed for causing his pain and bound to the Wounded Child; the Monster evolved as a means for the Wounded Child to take revenge on a cruel world, exerting his control and dominance.

> BH: Once you killed prostitutes, did you want to kill more?
> MJ: Yes, yes, definitely, because I couldn't bear them.

He killed his next victim, Millicent Smit, four months later. He chuckles as he tells me how he picked her up at a bar, then fooled her into following him some distance to a field. His voice becomes lower, sly, menacing, as he describes how he stripped her, then raped her. She begged not to be killed and he reassured her, then he strangled her while raping her, because, he says, she was making a racket. 'I was so quick. If it took two to three minutes, it was long. Two or three minutes, and you were gone.'

Michael, when in the character of the Monster, was street smart. As mentioned, he hung around at his murder scenes, watching how the police processed them. In the low, vengeful tone he uses when describing the murders, he says he overheard detectives 'talking shit' and thought, 'I'll show you.' The next murder, Michael said, was 'more professional': he removed the things they looked for and smeared butter on the soles of his feet to confuse the police dogs.

Describing why he murdered, Michael variously comments, 'I want to show God that I am God,' and, 'I do it to say, "I'm the president, ek roep [I call you]".' Michael issued these words like a medieval king, summoning a helpless subject to death. These are powerful expressions of his desire for ultimate control, for revenge.

It's striking how he blames others when in this character: it's his wife's fault for bringing the character of the Monster to life; it's the victims' fault for being sex workers. This character is a way to take revenge on those he imagines have wronged him: the Avenger-Monster.

Michael had meanwhile started a relationship with another woman, Natalie. For a time he drifted between Sarie and Natalie before divorcing Sarie in the early 1990s.

His relationship with Natalie was less obviously racked with conflict, but no less strange and tumultuous. Natalie reports Michael's unusual sexual preferences and demands, such as drinking her blood and trying to strangle her during sex. She had children from a previous relationship and she accused Michael of abusing them.

After this relationship broke down, Michael started to live in the dense seaside bush on the roadsides and on the hillsides of the city. The deep green of the bushes became the Monster's lair.

Eight months after Millicent's death, the Monster character transformed. In the same park where he had killed Millicent, he murdered a 14-year-old boy, sodomising him then strangling him with his own clothes. Although Michael is not always specific when talking about his victims, making more general statements about them, this is clearly another 'permutation' of the Monster character. Almost two years later, the decomposed body of another boy was found: a second male victim, left where Michael had killed before.

In both cases, Michael had propositioned the boys for sex, then killed them. Michael said that, generally, when the 'sex drive is high, the murder drive is high'.

There is the possibility that Michael killed children before this. It would not be inconsistent with the narrative he told or the character of the Monster. In our conversations Michael hints at crimes he may have committed before. Remember the strong circumstantial evidence linking him to Sam's death? Michael's disclosures are street smart, though: vividly clear on themes, they are vague on detail, so he doesn't incriminate himself too deeply.

Michael's story of why he murdered children is tangled and contrasting. He says repeatedly throughout his interview that if he saw people abuse a child, he would 'confiscate' that child. He frequently describes his killing of children as an act of mercy: 'I took them away so they wouldn't have to grow up with the things I had to.'

This permutation of Michael's Monster character was not an avenger but a saviour. It found abused children or, as Michael did not appear to know the boys he killed, children he presumed to be abused by virtue of their circumstances. He said he 'found a solution for the children, to kill them', then laments that he couldn't find a solution for himself, the story flowing back to his childhood abuse.

> BH: You didn't get the right help, and when you realised you couldn't trust people, the only way you could get this rage out was to murder?
> MJ: Precisely. Precisely.

In disorienting contrast to the motivation of the Saviour-Monster, Michael reports raping the children, and speaks of the pain he caused his child victims.

> When I was in that hostel and cried out for God, I wasn't helped. All the pain and screaming I felt, they felt ... I raped them. They cry out, cry out for God, like I did when I was raped. Then, in the process of raping them, I murder them, I kill them.

Michael associates this 'permutation' of the Monster powerfully with himself. Not only is his narration of killing children interwoven with images and tales of his own abuse; he now explicitly links the character to himself by giving it his own nickname: 'Takkies'.

> I went out as Takkies. I want to show God: you weren't there when I needed you. So I, I am God. I will preside over life and death. When doing these murders, I transformed, I became bigger ... Then later I transform back. Michael

returns to see what I've done, the corpse, and I take it and stick it away somewhere.

He left his female victims where they died 'because I hated them', but with his child victims, he hid the bodies in the bushes in secret places.

'I was tired after each murder. I had a resting place, because I couldn't go back home.' After a long pause, Michael says he had three 'resting places' he went to, after each murder, each two or three kilometres from where he committed his murders.

Michael says these murders are 'not easy for me to talk about'. He drank and did hard drugs to forget them. When under the influence of alcohol or drugs, though, he would murder again. 'It went on like that for a very long time, over years. It's why I say no one listens when you look for help.'

So now Michael was living with three different characters within him, all vying for control: the Wounded Child, never far from the surface, and always reminding him of his sense of unworthiness, loneliness and rejection; the Avenger-Monster, urging him to wreak terrible revenge on the women he blamed for deepening his pain; and the Saviour-Monster, punishing neglectful parents and 'saving' children by taking them away. Both permutations of the Monster gave him the control and dominance the Wounded Child could never get. Boiling beneath and between these characters were Michael's sexual needs, and the threatened transformation into the murderous Takkies when the tension got too much.

Ntombi Nkosi died in the grounds of a primary school. Her death was particularly brutal. 'I chewed on bits of them,' he chuckles, probably talking about her nipples, which he ate. 'I cut her open.' Calmly, he says he 'basically shoved his whole hand' into her and 'opened her up' with a knife. Then 'I left her there'. Leaving sex workers where they died was, for Michael, a sign of contempt.

His narration then becomes loaded with threat as he returns to descriptions of how he killed other sex workers. It's not always coherent, but the revenge and contempt are obvious.

We don't know precisely what caused the Avenger-Monster

character to return at this time. It may have been a result of his tumultuous home life, moving between Sarie and Natalie, living rough, and being accused of abusing children. What is clear, though, is that Michael's characters coexisted closely, able to express themselves suddenly.

During one of the frequent arguments and accusations that characterised his relationship with his ex-wife, Michael describes her saying that her new partner, Johan, had issued a particularly vile threat to her: 'If you don't have sex with me, I'll have sex with your daughter.' Melissa, 10 years old, was the child Sarie had had with Michael and Johan's threat threw Michael's internal world into disarray.

Michael went to fetch Melissa from her mother's house. He took her away in a taxi to a games arcade; he remembered being happy in arcades as a child. He questioned her.

> 'Did Johan fool about with you?' And she said, 'No, Dad. No, Dad.' 'Are you certain?' She said 'yes.' I didn't believe her, so I told her to take her panties off. She hesitated, so I pulled them off. I saw she was oop soos 'n volwassene vrou [open like a grown woman], so I killed my daughter. I killed her. So [voice rising] she would not have the same pain, the same grudge that I had, so she wouldn't do the same things I've done. In that moment, I became blind.

Michael again describes the pain he'd had as a child, asking what life is worth if you're not trusted, if you're a child, attacked and abused. 'It was pain, a grudge, it wasn't nice.'

> When I killed my little daughter, I felt relieved. She won't grow up like me. I saw to it that she was at peace. I didn't have sex with her. I just murdered her. So she won't grow up like me. Many people will wonder why I took my daughter away. They don't know. It was because she was raped. I didn't want her to grow up like I grew up. Maybe one day she would grow up to be a murderess, because her dad was a serial murderer.

Michael repeats how deeply, 'frighteningly', he loved his child.

> BH: Was that why you killed her?
> MJ: Yes. [Sighs]

Throughout his story, Michael says he killed children to stop them having the life he'd had; he insists he loved them and wanted to save them from that. The character of the Saviour-Monster, he says, saw parents mistreating children and then took them away from their suffering. But none of his victims really fitted this mould. Melissa insists she was not abused, and there is nothing to suggest Michael knew the family of any of the street children he murdered.

He tells me an anecdote of luring away the child of someone who had abused him as revenge. This may refer to his final victim, the only possible exception to the above pattern, perhaps the only victim Micheal saw being mistreated by his family.

Bobby Whitehead died in early 1997, the year Michael was arrested. Michael says he killed Bobby because the boy wasn't 'right' (maybe referring to learning difficulties), and alleges he was always hit and abused. He accuses Bobby's mother of being a 'whore', and always drunk. Michael says he saw how Bobby was treated with his own eyes, and threatened Bobby's mother with taking him away. 'I will take him … You must long for your child and for how he felt.' Rather than hurt her, Michael said he would take her child because it would hurt her more.

When he was raping Bobby, Michael reports, the jagged transformation came on him.

> BH: When the sex drive is high, the murder urge came with the sex urge?
> MJ: Spot on.

This led to his arrest and then swiftly to his confession.

Michael frequently comments how murder 'makes you tired, very tired. It exhausts you.'

> BH: Tired of yourself, the world?
> MJ: Tired of everything. Tired of everything.

This wasn't the reason he confessed, though. The reason he gives for exposing his secret, claustrophobic world to the light is, 'I decided to work with the police to protect children.' This strange comment, as if his confession was an act of child protection, makes sense when considered in the context of his fractured internal characters. What started as a single character split, from Wounded Child to Monster, then split again, into the permutations of the Monster, with each permutation's motives splitting again. Like the fractals of a crystal, each character stood isolated from the others.

The leaping of his spoken narrative from abuse to murder, from revenge to saviour, doesn't just demonstrate what motivated Michael and how he justified his own behaviour. It reveals a hidden pattern in his story: an inner disintegration. His story is an example of the harm that can be caused when the narrative of the inner characters disintegrates. It ultimately allowed Michael, in the guise of the Saviour-Monster, to murder children and so avenge himself on abusive parents, to 'save' children from a life of abuse, to 'show God' by making them scream, and to satisfy a sexual urge strongly linked to murder – all at the same time, fractured and contradictory.

This didn't seem to be a case of split personalities, and he wasn't diagnosed with anything like dissociative personality disorder. This was more subtle. The mythical horror creature was simply a story filled with disintegrated characters, all in sharp contradiction to each other, and unreconciled in his story. This enabled him to continue offending without inner conflict; the split let him be saviour, and victim, and molester, and murderer, all at once.

Michael got to meet his biological family for the first time after he was imprisoned. He describes greeting his biological mother for the first time with a childlike 'Mommy'. Meeting them and speaking with them and understanding more about his past (not just through the broken glass of his own narratives) seems to have helped him deal with the fundamental pain he suffered, easing the feeling that he was a child who had been 'thrown away'. Maybe if he addressed that, he could start to untangle the visceral link between sex, pain and murder that rose within him in a jagged transformation.

This is the fourth killer story: disintegration, with the inner story splitting into sharp separation between characters. Every conflict in life creates another split and each split allows killing to start, and continue, unimpeded by insight or remorse.

5 Sarel: The other, outside

The crimes

During the 1980s and 1990s, a wave of fear spread through the United States. Whispers of ritual murder and abuse soon grew to hysterical levels as ordinary Americans became convinced that satan-worshipping groups were attempting to take over their country. No one was safe from these groups of people. Pets, babies and virgin girls were being sacrificed at the altar of dark forces. It was a holy war between good and evil.

Except, it wasn't. There was no evil, occultic threat on the horizon, but the 'satanic panic' era would become an excellent example of how even those who should have been intent on quashing such things instead fuelled it. Government and even law-enforcement bodies in the United States helped to support the panic by buying into it almost as wholeheartedly as citizens. Police officers were trained in the identification of satanic murders. Politicians spoke of the war against evil in their election bids: if you weren't overtly in the battle, you were clearly one of 'them'. And, of course, the hysteria was fuelled by the mainstream media assigning a 'satanic' label to almost every crime with strange circumstances.

Thankfully, sanity would eventually prevail. The claims were debunked one by one, and the satanic panic era would become just another phase, remembered with more than a little embarrassment as a moment in time when logic went out the window.

South Africa then was a very different place from today. The National Party was in power and the apartheid regime was in force, but the majority of South Africans were pushing back. The government, feeling its grip on power slipping, looked for any opportunity to maintain its hold. If that meant harnessing fear, it was not above it.

When satanic panic hit the shores of South Africa, it was almost immediately seized as a weaponised form of control by politicians intent on maintaining the status quo. The National Party added 'satanism' to the things that white people should fear, alongside black people and communism. It used this additional layer of fear to try to ensure that white people clung to the status quo to protect themselves. Before long, the possibility that a black majority may ever gain control in South Africa became synonymous with satanic panic – at least in the minds of some white South Africans.

The history of South Africa's white population as a whole also made it fertile ground for fear-based narratives of this kind. Whether it was the Great Trek, the Boer War or the South African government choosing to back the Allies in the two World Wars, it made for a background filled with instances of real or perceived affronts by 'evil' forces. It made complete sense that this narrative would carry over into the satanic panic era.

Although South Africa became a democracy in 1994, those who lived through that time still bore scars from the past, including the conditioning of fear-mongering, both race-based and religious in nature. Like a hidden birthmark, this conditioning had been passed down through generations of South Africans, and the fear had remained as a smouldering ember just waiting for kindling. As a result, South Africa never quite expelled satanic panic entirely. Every time a bizarre murder occurred or a perpetrator attempted to claim external influences beyond their control, the flame reignited for a time.

At the height of the panic, it was not uncommon for church leaders to issue parents lists of instructions to protect their children from satanic influence. Certain types of music, cartoons and clothing were all deemed evil, banned from homes and burned in gardens under the murmured chant of the Lord's Prayer. Schools were a natural choice to secure the spiritual safety of children: assemblies were taken over by police officers from the SAP's Occult-Related Crime Unit or individuals who'd taken it on themselves to warn children about satanism.

The irony of this is that often children who had never even thought about occult practices were suddenly introduced to this dark and, for many, interesting world: if the adults were prohibiting them from it, that must mean there was something to see, right? For many South African children, an interest in the occult would be a passing phase, but for at least one young boy at this time, standing in his oversized blazer in the echoey hall of his boarding school, it would be just the thing his already struggling mind sought.

The crimes in this case are different from others discussed in this book for a few reasons. First, they were not serial in nature in the way we might expect; and, second, there were two perpetrators involved, although both were not involved in all the crimes. Also, all the victims survived.

The police in the area in which this criminal pairing would operate did not tie these crimes together immediately. This is despite the crimes in question occurring over the space of less than a year, all in the same area, and, on closer inspection, with some similarities that appeared to come from the modus operandi of one of the pair.

In the early 1990s, in the business district of a coastal town, a young woman was abducted outside a shopping centre. She would later describe to police how the perpetrator had appeared at her open car window, flashed a weapon, and ordered her to move into the passenger seat. In an hours-long ordeal, the young victim was driven around the town and its outskirts. On two occasions, the man, whom she would come to know as Koen Bosman, had stopped the car and raped her.

She had tried multiple methods to get the man to release her: she had cried, begged for her life, and eventually activated what is known as the 'fawn' response, in which she had tried to make

Bosman see her as a friend. None of these efforts seemed to have any impact on the man, and the violence and terror had continued.

Bizarrely, towards the end of her ordeal, Bosman had purchased food and gifts for her. He had then driven her to a desolate spot, raped her again, and finally released her.

The young victim in this case was terrified and did not immediately report the rape. About a week later, she broke down and admitted the story to a friend, who insisted she report the crime to the police.

Hesitation to report is not uncommon with rape victims – according to a 2008 report co-published by the South African Medical Research Council, only one in nine rapes is reported in South Africa. But this first recorded incident in this series displays another important background aspect: sexual assault with foreign objects, anal penetration, and digital or oral rape were not yet legally classified as rape (this happened only in 2007). Neither the public nor even legal professionals properly understood the role of coercion in rape and the nuances around consent. Perhaps the best example of the deep lack of understanding around the crime of rape during this time is that marital rape (the rape of a spouse or domestic partner) was then not a criminal act. South Africa passed the law pertaining to marital rape only in 2000.

This societal and legal attitude towards rape would underpin both the victims' traumas and the perpetrators' attitudes toward their crimes and it is important as a backdrop in this series of crimes.

Koen Bosman was arrested for this first crime after the victim went to the police. He was released on bail of R100. This is perhaps more shocking because Bosman's crime was not 'only' rape: he had abducted his victim at gunpoint and held her against her will for hours.

Several months after this crime, another abduction and rape occurred. The woman later testified that two men approached her on the road. One pointed a gun at her and forced her to walk with them. She was taken to a second location and raped by both men. She said that the perpetrators discussed killing her, but ultimately decided to let her go.

As she fled the scene, she spotted a police van, flagged it down, and gave them a description and the last location of the pair. Police officers searched the area and spotted two men on foot. The victim identified them as her attackers. The men – Koen Bosman and his newly acquired partner in crime, Sarel van der Spuy – were arrested and charged with rape.

In yet another shocking failure of justice, Bosman's existing rape case (and his awaiting-trial status) didn't flag with the police. He had violated the terms of his bail by being accused of and arrested for another crime, and should never have been released. Nevertheless, both were let out on bail.

Just two weeks later, on an isolated road on the other side of town, a young man made a horrific discovery in the early hours of the morning. He slowed his vehicle as he noticed blood smeared across the tar. He briefly considered someone may have hit an animal, but then saw the source of the blood: in a crumpled heap on the road lay the naked body of a young woman.

An ambulance rushed the woman to hospital. She had sustained devastating injuries. The admitting doctor said he hadn't seen such injuries to a living human being in his 15 years of practice. She had also been raped.

Her survival was miraculous, and her tenacity and strength would prove to be lifesaving for many more potential victims. The information she gave the police in the hours after the attack ensured that she did not become the first in a series of potential murders, but, rather, the one who would finally put two violent individuals behind bars.

The victim had been abducted by one of the perpetrators on arrival at her home in her car in the early hours of the morning. He had held a gun to her head and forced her to move over to the passenger seat. He'd then driven to a collect a second perpetrator.

The first perpetrator had initially given her a fake name, but she'd heard the second man call him Koen. A female police officer who had worked on Koen Bosman's first rape case immediately suspected that it was he who had committed this crime too. Sure enough, as soon as the photo lineup was placed in front of the victim, still in her hospital bed, she pointed directly at him.

While several police units set out in search of Bosman, the victim relayed the rest of the details of the bizarre and terrifying attack to a detective, including comments the men had made about devil worship and sacrifices. This would become a major theme in the case and, of course, the satanic panic-ready South African public picked up the occult baton once again – and there was no stopping the rumour mill.

Bosman was swiftly arrested and he gave up Sarel van der Spuy's name, which led to his arrest too. Police officers said both men expressed shock on hearing they were being charged with attempted murder. They had perhaps been certain their victim would never have survived the injuries they'd inflicted.

Both were found guilty of the charges against them – including the other rapes – and were handed down life sentences.

Sarel's killer story

Sarel is polite and eager to help. If I interrupt, he stops talking and waits for me to finish. When we take a break and I forget to stop the tape recording, he presses 'pause' for me.

He has dark brown wide-set eyes and a broad, friendly smile. I almost immediately compare myself to him. We're both in our early twenties; only a year separates us in age. His hair is slightly longer than my short back and sides, and lighter brown. He has heavy stubble and a thin moustache. His clothing seems less like the usual prison uniform: a camouflage vest under prison overalls. He has a silver ring on his right hand and a white triangular tooth on a leather thong around his neck.

His prison tattoos strike a darker tone: a column of images, of a long-haired skull, the anarchy symbol, and twin smoking guns march down his left arm. On his other arm, the horror doll Chucky sits with eyes and mouth sewn shut, hair wild. A Chinese dragon lunges across his back.

The inside of his left arm is scarred by accidents, barbed-wire fences and a self-inflicted slash. There is a large scar on the back of his left hand where he had used rock salt to rub away a demon tattoo; 'It was badly done,' he explains.

I think that he – goodlooking, muscled and compact – would have been popular in the student nightclubs back in the university town where I lived. Chatting to him feels like chatting to a peer. He switches easily between English and Afrikaans, and our closeness in age and his familiarity make me especially keen to maintain rapport.

As he warms up over the course of two days, his arms unfold and his naturally comical storytelling style emerges. He has a sharp memory. He recalls names easily, and even remembers the flavour of the late-night snack he bought on the evening of his worst crime. When I ask a question, he cocks his head to the side and squints at me, scrunching his eyes up as if looking into the sun. When he thinks about his responses, especially when talking about relationship breakups, he pauses in heavy silence, staring up or down to the left, his eyes far away, clenching his fist. Talking about them upsets him: 'When girlfriends left, I felt there was still a part of them left in me.'

He wishes sincerely that he could have a family. Mirroring the contrast between his smile and his tattoos, his longing for the community of family life is counterbalanced by his prodigious interest in the occult. He says the occult definitely contributed to his committing his crime.

Sarel grew up in a forest paradise in one of the most strikingly beautiful parts of South Africa. His earliest memories are of running under trees on a farm, playing cars in the shade and seeing monkeys behind the garage.

His boyhood, though, was dominated by his stepfather, 'the Baboon'. The nickname was bestowed on account of his constant shouting, like an aggressive male primate from a rocky outcrop. Sarel's stepfather was a driver in the forestry service and had not completed high school. Sarel describes him as strict and inflexible and the conflict between them as a constant.

Even to this day, I don't like being screamed at because

if that person screams at me, I see my stepdad. It's him standing there screaming at me.

Sarel was illegitimate, something he was never told about until an aunt, commenting on the fighting with his stepfather, commented, 'You know he's not your real dad, don't you?' Though his mother tried to protect him, this made the relationship with his stepfather worse still. Sarel eavesdropped on a conversation between them and heard himself being described as 'the only fuckup' in their relationship.

His mother was a warm-hearted and soft-natured solace and supporter for the young Sarel, who had been born to her in later life, the product of a short-lived relationship while she was working in a local supermarket. As Sarel wryly comments, 'They jumped into bed, and I popped out.' His mother never let his biological father know of his birth. Sarel questions how a 'real father' would have handled his growing up, although when I met him, he had not sought out his biological father. Sarel admitted that, after all, the man was in prison for drug smuggling.

Sarel was very protective of his mother. If his stepfather had ever touched her, he says, 'I would have killed him.' As if to emphasise the point, Sarel describes an incident when he was eight years old, and he struck a girl his age who was rude to his mother. His mother, like his girlfriends, is a source of comfort in the hostile external world and has his devoted commitment.

Sarel's family were poor, their life a sharp contrast to the prosperity of nearby towns. They had no electricity, he recalls, and lived by the light of paraffin lamps. His evenings were spent chopping or collecting wood for the family fire, and being shouted at by the Baboon for cutting pieces incorrectly or not collecting enough.

Sarel started to attend boarding school as a relief from the 'stress atmosphere' at home. He loved boarding school. The tales from this time in his life are comical, full of his light-hearted mischief and pranks. He reported having good friends and his first sexual experiences, and, at the end of primary school, his first girlfriend, Belinda. He says she was his first real love.

While Sarel reports having had many girlfriends, he seems to have been deeply emotionally committed to each. They become support and comfort, and his descriptions of their relationships are enthusiastic, filled with emotion.

His home life was still stressful, though. School holidays were spent cutting wood, cleaning, riding bakkies: 'There are no discos in the bush,' Sarel quips. His mother's two much older daughters from a previous marriage were no comfort for Sarel when they came to stay, and he felt that they were intruding on his life, pushing him aside. This sense of powerlessness obviously gnawed at the youngster.

At around the same time he met Belinda, the other relationship in his life was kindled when a police officer visited their school to talk about the dangers of the occult. For an adolescent rebelling, wondering why people didn't treat him well, and wanting freedom, the occult sounded intoxicating.

> You get power. You get power there which other people
> don't have. That's what I searched for, and I got it.

The occult, and later satanism, gave him another way to handle the 'pressure at home', and being 'powerless' against his stepfather, unable to take revenge on him.

> I asked God to give me strength, he didn't give me strength.
> I went to the occult, and then I got strength.

As Sarel grew older, the influence of the occult and the influence of his girlfriends shaped his narrative more and more.

When he was 14, Sarel's stepfather tried to assault him sexually. He had encouraged Sarel to take a nap on the bed with him, listening to the family radio in his room. Sarel had dozed off, waking to find his stepfather attempting to molest him. Sarel struck his stepfather in the face, pushing him away. Afterwards, his stepfather brought in coffees for them both and asked him not to tell his mother.

Later, at night, Sarel went to find his stepfather's gun. He loaded and cocked it, and stood over his sleeping stepfather. He was about to pull the trigger, then stopped. 'I don't know what prevented me,' he says.

Sarel went on to ambush his stepfather as he sat on the toilet, attacking him with a pickaxe handle. He says that his anger was fuelled not only by the assault on him, but by his stepfather's molestation of a niece and how his mother had been affected by this. (Sarel never said how he came to know of the assault on the girl, or how his mother was affected.) His attacking his stepfather was, he says, his way of trying to 'handle' this. It seemed to satiate his desire for revenge. He said he didn't hate his stepfather, just 'couldn't understand him at all', especially his refusal to discuss things relationally.

You can see the most powerful characters in Sarel's story emerge at this stage in his narrative: The Girlfriends and The Occult. These characters share a common purpose with the characters we've seen in previous killer stories: they offered Sarel a way to deal with the circumstances life threw at him.

The Girlfriends character is a source of comfort and a reminder to Sarel that he is loved. Perhaps the inner character of The Girlfriends evolved from his devotion to his mother or perhaps it is the product of the affirmation Sarel got from his young relationships. Whatever the source, The Girlfriends connected Sarel with other people and with a sense of community.

The Occult character seemed to spring from the opposite pressure, as a way for Sarel to deal with his feelings of helplessness in the face of the Baboon and his emerging anger and resentment at how society treated him. The Occult offered Sarel a feeling of power and control that was otherwise lacking.

Together, these two became pivotal characters in his story, steering the way he behaved and managed his life.

Sarel went from the hostel to a school in the north of the country, where he stayed with one of his sisters. His sister 'didn't know how to handle boys', apparently – not that he misbehaved, insisted Sarel, just that she didn't know how to 'sit and talk, and find out what bothered me'. So, after about a year, he was sent away and told he couldn't return.

His mother then found a place for him at a school in another city. For Sarel, going to different schools was an adventure. 'New faces, new oldies,' he laughs. The light-hearted prankster he reports being at school was becoming aware, however, of how poor his family was compared to those of his school mates. He had to borrow sports equipment from other children, and his mother and stepfather never travelled to the school for sports days due to a reported lack of money.

The richer children, the sons and daughters of local farmers, were snobbish towards Sarel. He initially claims not to have been unduly bothered by this, as he had the companionship of another so-called 'boskind' (bush child), a poor kid from the forests like him.

Sarel, however, railed against his place in the social order of his school. 'People were always calling me bad, or dirty,' he says, and he wanted to break free of that, of the label of 'boskind'. The Occult gave him that. It helped him to overcome his sense of powerlessness in the society of which he was part.

Moving from school to school, Sarel reports repeatedly bumping into other children who were satanists. He describes collecting satanic books, having strange visions in the night, and a memorable tryst with a mysterious woman involving occult paraphernalia and her vanishing (along with the occult trappings) when morning came.

The character of The Occult seems relatively benign at this stage, a hobby that gave Sarel a sense of belonging and control. He admits, though, that satanism was a 'wrong idea'.

As this stage, The Girlfriends were far more influential. Sarel has been speaking about how he never believed in hurting women or raping them, then, in increasingly passionate and engaged tones, he describes how the purpose of life is for people to have relationships and to enter into relationships – 'that is the reason there are two genders, men and women, because one seeks the other'.

Sarel's descriptions of his relationships are the emotional high points of his story. He is a romantic. Describing his relationships, his tone becomes intense. He has to pause frequently, overcome by emotion.

While Sarel says he had many girlfriends, there were two that stood out. Anna and Cathy dominated his late teens. He describes meeting Anna first, liking her unusual eyes and her personality. Although he reports that they went out for only three to five months, their bond was a close one. He said he 'really wanted to get to know her, more than anyone else'. They parted when he left her town and she said a long-distance relationship couldn't work.

Later, Sarel would go AWOL from the army (he had been conscripted) to go and find her. He describes standing on sentry duty one night, feeling overwhelmed – 'I still had feelings for her, it didn't matter what happened' – and abandoning his post to go on the run to her home town. He got caught by the military police before he found her – although, in a coincidence worthy of a movie, Anna's mother bumped into him after he was arrested and told him that Anna had left for a job in another town.

After his time in the army, Sarel moved to a coastal town and found work with a security company, and later for a salt company. He seems to have got on well with his work colleagues: 'If I work, I work. I am not lazy.'

Cathy was 15 when she met the 19-year-old Sarel. He thought that if he couldn't get Anna, then he needed to get someone else, a 'replacement', and Cathy looked like Anna: 'same personality, same character.' He had seen her around the area he hung out in and invited her to a party, giving her drinks on the side. He describes helping her study, motivating her to work, forgiving her when she snuck out to party at a disco. He would pick her up from school, walk her home and make sure she did her homework.

For her 16th birthday a friend gave Cathy brandy as a gift, and she got very drunk. Sarel said it was 'my job, my duty, to keep her safe; as her boyfriend'. He got her home and into bed. They slept separately, and he laughingly describes her hangover the next day, before tailing off into nostalgic silence. 'It was good times.'

Sarel had woven Cathy into his life plan. He describes having planned to finish national service, then join the air force and work in security. While he completed his army service, the other goals were adjusted to fit with his waiting for Cathy to finish high school.

He wanted to marry her. But it was not to be. She broke up with him after they had been going out for five months.

Sarel blames 'rumours', protesting that he did nothing wrong: 'I kept my part of the deal … I put my head on this one. I gave everything to her. We had a good relationship,' he laments, before lapsing into a long silence.

It is striking how brief his relationships with Anna and Cathy were – a handful of months each – yet how they take absolute priority. The two women seem to merge into a single person in Sarel's story; often, I struggle to discern which one he is talking about. He seems deeply committed to each, though, a romantic throwing himself into his relationships with The Girlfriends with complete abandon: he runs away from the army, risks imprisonment, commits to marriage. He still struggles to speak about the breakup of his relationships.

He wishes he could have spoken to Cathy to understand why she left, saying the end of the relationship still bothers him terribly and he wants a better picture of why it happened. He says he can't get rid of his feelings for her or resolve them.

> I really struggled to cope with some of my emotions. I tried
> to deal with these things in one way. This is how I ended up
> in prison.

Cathy, he says, had a nervous breakdown when he got arrested.

Sarel's struggle to deal with the breakup of this relationship was 'where things started to go wrong. They started to run off course …'

Up to this point, the external influences of The Girlfriends and The Occult seemed to operate separately. However, the break-up of this relationship signalled the start of The Occult becoming his sole focus. Without the influence of The Girlfriends calling on him to devote himself to others, the influence of The Occult calling on him to grab power ran riot.

> SV: Why did I do it? In my case, there are many factors. A
> girl left me. I got in a predicament with her stepfather
> and rolled his work bakkie, which meant I had to pay
> for damages, R3 000, which I didn't have. I decided

> I was tired. How come I say I don't hate women? I say it because the things I did against women weren't personal.
>
> BH: What was it?
>
> SV: It was because they were part of the life and community, and I wanted to hit it back for all the hard times they had given me.

Echoing the lonely isolation of previous killer stories, Sarel says he had all these problems but did not know who to speak to about them: there 'wasn't anyone there to help me deal with these problems'.

By this stage, Sarel says he had been a satanist for almost a decade. He had met many fellow satanist or occult people at school or in the army. This, Sarel says, needs to be considered when thinking about his crimes. These factors, he says, placed him at the heart of a spiritual war between good and evil.

> I was young. It was a fight between the devil and God. Because we were young, we were used, like in a chess game. [Stutteringly] People that don't know the occult don't understand. They look at the crime, not deeper, into what caused the crime. [When someone commits a crime with an occult factor, they] mustn't just punish them; they [must] get a psychologist and must sit with them so they can understand. If there's a suggestion of the occult, then you must sit down with the child and ask them what's wrong, and when they tell you, you must believe them. They are speaking the truth. They aren't talking big; they are speaking the truth.

This last includes, says Sarel, when someone says they feel like they are possessed, unable to remember or control what they are doing. When we fail to help these people, he insists, it is a crime, 'a murder'.

Sarel talks about spiritual warfare, painting himself as a pawn in the battle between the towering supernatural forces of good and evil. He simultaneously tangentially criticises the lack of help he received as a child struggling under occult influences. By placing the accountability for his crimes outside himself, in an external character, he lessens his responsibility. How could a human being be expected to stand against such a power?

This signals a change in his inner character of The Occult. Triggered by the loss of his girlfriend, the pressures of life and his simmering resentment against society, it becomes more powerful and deadly. The inner character transforms from The Occult to Satanism. Sarel starts to speak of human sacrifice. He says that he had wanted to sacrifice a woman to get greater occult powers. He says he wasn't interested merely in raping and killing; he wanted a human sacrifice under demonic influence so he could 'go up a rung' in the satanic church.

That all went wrong, he says, when the person he committed his crimes with 'lost it'.

Sarel's meeting Koen Bosman could not have come at a worse time. Sarel was struggling emotionally from his breakup, unable to handle his feelings, and Koen helped magnify his interest in the occult. Koen had been involved in the occult since he was 13 years old. Koen, Sarel reports, claimed he had been hexed and assigned a demon called Incubus.

Sarel had known Koen for only three or four months before they committed rape together. He says they got on well and didn't argue. Like with Anna and Cathy, it seems that Sarel was swept along by a relationship that chimed closely with his inner characters.

> BH: You said you didn't hate women. Did Koen hate women?
> SV: Yes, and he had a nice girlfriend, Amanda. I would have liked to have Amanda myself. She adored him and did everything for him but he didn't treat her well. I didn't like how he treated Amanda – like a slave, I told him, but it was his wife. I didn't know why Koen treated her so badly and used her as a sex tool.

Sarel says Koen ordered her to have sex with Sarel, or else she would 'be in trouble'. 'What sort of man tells his wife to do that?' Sarel exclaims. He objected to the lack of respect, to Koen's treating his wife as a prostitute or an object. She was upset, and 'when [Koen] was gone, I told her not to worry about it, just leave it'.

g his trial, Sarel said he developed feelings for
:d seeing her in court.

> uld forget her but I couldn't. I would have her
> ..... any day, any day. I sometimes wonder how things
> are going for her.

Koen had already, unknown to Sarel, raped a woman called Zoë. Sarel says that Koen was obsessed with the actress Michelle Pfeiffer and had a book of pictures of her. Koen's first victim looked like her, Sarel reports.

> Koen had wanted to rape someone who looked like
> Michelle Pfeiffer. He hurt the women who didn't look like
> Michelle Pfeiffer. That's my opinion of the case, that I saw.

Sarel supplies the following narrative of the rape of Zoë, which he says Koen told him after their arrest. Koen had been in a bar. He had masturbated in the toilets, then gone outside to go home. He had spotted 19-year-old Zoë sitting in her car. He knew Zoë, as they frequented the same disco. She had just finished a work shift in a restaurant and was busy counting her earnings. Koen had his .22 pistol with him and 'he pointed the pistol through the window, jumped in the car, [told Zoë to shift over] and rode off', Sarel says, snapping his fingers on the last phrase to show how quick and effective Koen had been in this abduction.

Koen had driven the car to a nearby town. There, he had given Zoë a rose and apparently said, 'We are in lover's lane now. I am the first rapist to give you a rose.' He had raped her there, then driven to the beach, where he had bought dagga. He had smoked this with Zoë, then had raped her again. Koen had then dropped her off and gone home to his wife.

Sarel says Koen told him he was awaiting trial for the case, but the case kept being delayed because Zoë was using drugs a lot and was 'los' [promiscuous]. Sarel acknowledges, proactively, that this was just Koen's version and may not be true.

In the weeks preceding the first crime for which he was imprisoned, the seeming satanic influence over Sarel intensified, mirroring the closer synchronisation of action with Koen. Saying that he, too, has a demon, like Koen's Incubus, he adds that now, in prison, he would want an exorcism but there is no one there to help him and do it properly: 'They just pray and light a few candles' and that's not an exorcism, he says. 'It needs to be a fight.'

Sarel describes the weeks and days before the rape of their first victim, Mienkie, as an otherworldly experience.

> At this stage I wasn't worried about where I was going and what I was doing. For three days before this happened, I felt like a zombie, like something had taken me over and I could only half-think. One side was dead. I just had half control over my body.

Sarel describes shovelling salt at work, when suddenly something started coming out of the air and entering him, snatching his breath away. Then came the electricity, 'like I was on an upper', and he felt full of energy, not wanting to stop working.

Later, a cold feeling and a pain in his stomach began.

> I perceived there was something inside me, starting to apply pressure. I had no control over feelings, and felt dead. I felt like a zombie. The voice said, 'You must go drink.'

He went to find a beer to ease the pain. He was with Koen and he didn't go back to work.

Koen noticed the change in Sarel, as did others.

> SV: People got scared of me. I got cold. They spoke, and I just stared at them.
> BH: What happened?
> SV: I was turning black. I felt that if I didn't wear black, I'd be exposed. To this day, I wear black. If I don't, I'll be seen; the people will see me.

Sarel believes these changes were due to the occult. He felt changes in his behaviour: a powerful desire to hurt, particularly when he saw Christians in the street. 'I felt challenged by them. It was as if something came from deep in my stomach and flowed over me,' he says, his voice filling with intensity. Sarel says he still avoids speaking to Christians in the prison, avoiding and disliking them; while he is saying this, his voice deepens eerily, huskily, making the hairs on my neck stand up. Then he coughs, clears his throat and speaks about his struggles being due to not just psychological factors, but also (his voice returning to its more familiar tone) the spiritual war going on both inside him and around him. 'I don't have control over it. Things happen on a spiritual level, and I can't say what.'

This illustrates the influence of the character of Satanism in Sarel's narrative. It contributes to the sense that his feelings are being overwhelmed by a powerful force from outside, as if he is led from outside himself. At the very least, his normal emotions are overwhelmed, so he wanders zombie-like into crime.

There is perhaps another more subtle function of this narrative device. By casting himself as the victim of a malignant, over-whelming supernatural influence, Sarel also lessens the focus on the horror of the victims and so perhaps, in his mind, the severity of what he and Koen did.

Sarel says that Koen wanted to rape more, after his crime against Zoë. He contrasts this with himself, who 'doesn't like this thing'.

> If I hadn't gone with Koen, I wouldn't have committed the crimes. If I was out alone, the offences wouldn't have happened. I like women. I would never had done it.

It's difficult to say whether Sarel's reports of regret and hesitation in committing the crime are accurate, or a justification after the event. I tend to believe Sarel's claims for not wanting to commit rape. He did not report any interest in rape beforehand and he repeatedly tries to draw parallels with 'normal' sex. More compellingly, though, committing rape was at sharp odds with what satanism required of him: kidnap and sacrifice.

There is a difference between sacrificing a young and an old person, he explains: the young person is sacrificed to get power; an adult is more of a homage. He insists that Koen and his whole motive for kidnapping a woman was to have a sacrifice.

> SV: You know, if you are doing a sacrifice, the woman must be pretty. From 14, 13, 10 years old. She must be

> beautiful ... Those were the messages we got from
> the demons: 'kidnap someone, and sacrifice that
> person.'
>
> BH: How did these messages come?
> SV: Koen told me. He got these messages from Incubus.
> Whenever he told me about the messages from
> Incubus, I would hear his voice in my head too. When
> he said his name, there was a cold thing that came
> over my whole body, like cold water poured over my
> head. [It] was a weird feeling.

Mienkie's kidnap and rape happened quite suddenly. It was late on a summer night.

> BH: What made you decide to do this?
> SV: It was curiosity. Life was boring. It was a Saturday
> night and sometimes you don't want to go to parties.
> I was bored. I was lying in bed, and Koen woke me
> up. He wore black. He said, 'We need to go now.' It
> was instinct that made me wear pitch black. When we
> were ready, he said, 'We need to go get a woman and
> rape her.' 'Why?' I asked. 'Because we will get powers.'

He said Koen was speaking in a confused way, making it hard to understand him. Sarel considered it a demonic attack, which is, according to him, a 'test of faith'. It was after midnight, and over the next three hours the duo roved the streets, carrying a BB gun, on foot across the whole city centre. One potential victim was spotted, then swiftly rejected.

> We found this short little girl by the side of the road. Koen
> said, 'Leave her, I work with her,' so we let her go.

They walked on for, Sarel figures, three or four kilometres, when they found Mienkie.

> We saw this Arabian-looking girl in the street. It was about
> 2.30, 3 am. It was quiet in the street, there was no one
> there.

Sarel didn't feel she was the right woman, complaining that her bearing and presentation weren't 'quite right'. Still, they followed her.

> Then the demon Incubus said to [Koen], 'Now's the time. If you don't do it, you will die.' Koen looked crazy. Mad, mad. He wanted to kill her. He put the gun in her ribs, and she got a big shock. She handed over her handbag, and I walked with it for a while.

Sarel made a point of saying he never stole anything from the handbag. Mienkie asked for a cigarette and they gave her one. They climbed over a fence into a park and sat on the grass. Sarel and Koen sat either side of Mienkie.

> BH: Was she afraid?
> SV: She was nervous, tense, stiff.

It strikes me as odd that Sarel doesn't seem to want to admit his victims were afraid or hurt. Just as Satanism relieved him of the moral burden of his actions, it also seemed to minimise their suffering and his own responsibility for causing it.

Koen started playing with Mienkie's breasts. He encouraged Sarel to do the same, so he reluctantly touched her and then stopped. He then 'looked at the city lights, because it was pretty there, and listened to the noise of the people below, in the club'.

Koen asked Mienkie for fellatio but she declined. Koen then said to Sarel, 'Now you must have sex with her first.'

> So she undressed and stuff, and I had sex with her. I kissed her, she kissed me back, and she gave me a love bite on my neck. When I was finished, I got dressed again, and went and lay on the grass a short distance away. Then Koen had sex with her. I looked once. He had sex with her in a vicious way so I didn't look again. I looked into the air. She sat and shivered; she got cold so she put clothes on.

Mienkie's shivering may have been due to shock rather than the cold.

Sarel's reflections seem to minimise the act of rape, implying it may have been less serious than it was.

> Well, it was intimate, because she kissed me back. It didn't
> feel like rape. She didn't push me away, she cooperated.

He found Mienkie's cooperation, kissing him back and giving him a love bite 'weird'. I asked why she may have done this, thinking to myself that having been kidnapped at gunpoint by two strange men in a deserted city centre might have meant Mienkie was just thinking of her survival. Sarel did not answer directly, returning to the strangeness of it feeling like a 'married relationship'.

After he had raped her, Koen said to Sarel, 'Now we have to kill the woman.' Sarel tells me, 'Then I said no, it's Christmas, it's the festive season, leave her and let her go.'

Sarel's sense of being absent emotionally, in a way he never had before, persists throughout this event.

> I didn't feel myself. I felt numb, like a zombie, like a switch
> had been flicked and a light had gone off.

These feelings of coldness, numbness and loss of emotion were strongly associated with the character of Satanism in Sarel's narrative. They signified his being overwhelmed, by both the character's influence and the circumstances. When Sarel was being led by these outside entities, perhaps cutting off his emotions was the only way he could continue to effectively function.

Koen told Mienkie that she could go home. He said she mustn't tell anyone, Sarel recalls, or they would come back and kill her children.

As he and Koen walked away down the street, slowly, Sarel's emotions returned. But the feelings of coldness and numbness would come before their next crime.

> I felt like another thing came out, did its thing, and then
> withdrew. Then the other person comes slowly back in.

It wasn't long before the police caught them: Mienkie had flagged down a patrol car and given them a description. Arrested, bailed, the police seemingly unaware of Koen's previous rape accusation, the two men were soon free again.

After Mienkie's rape, says Sarel, Koen started to follow women in the street. The two men began hanging around a shopping mall to find the right woman to kidnap. Sarel comments ruefully that while 'I had an idea in my head about the type of person to kidnap, [Koen] just wanted to kidnap anyone, and that's not what it's about'.

When I ask how long they searched for women, Sarel counts the days very precisely, accounting for when they had to work. It was only a few days before they committed their final crime.

The crimes happened in the moment, with no planning in advance. There were a couple of attempted kidnappings from the shopping-mall carpark, near-misses for prospective victims. They watched a redhead get into a car; Sarel pointed her out, Koen went over and tried the door, but she locked it and sped off. They watched one of Sarel's co-workers walk past them. Spotting another woman, Koen commented 'she's working on my case'; unaware of the rape he had committed against Zoë, Sarel didn't know what Koen meant. Another attempted kidnapping went wrong when their victim was saved by passersby.

'The whole mission was a flop. That evening, Koen was very angry,' says Sarel.

Sarel then started to suffer the same strange symptoms he had before Mienkie's rape, only more severe this time: 'like you switch on a robot, [and] the electrical power flows through them.' Describing it as 'demons', he says,

> I knew what I was doing [but] I had no control over my actions, I had no reaction to my actions. It's as if I was paralysed. I had tunnel vision.

Marissa's rape and attempted murder happened about two weeks – 'nine days, fifteen days', estimates Sarel – after Mienkie's rape. There was a full moon on the night of the crime and Sarel says the temperature veered between hot and cold, and he lost track of time. 'It felt like a hundred years. It was a fight between the devil and God that night.'

They started the warm summer evening the same way as young people do all over the country, having a braai. Then they began drinking cough mixture for the buzz it gave them.

Later, Koen and Sarel headed out on foot to find a woman. They were both carrying knives. They sat next to a traffic light, waiting for an appropriate victim to drive past. To Sarel's annoyance, Koen feel asleep.

> 'Hey, wake up, bra,' I said to him. 'Do you think I will shoot a woman in her car alone? No, man, you're mad. I'm going to leave.' He said, 'No, no, I'll show you. I will go get a woman; I'll go get one alone.' But he was drunk as a skunk and could barely stand, but there he goes. I said I was going to go and started to walk.

Sarel walked to a service station, buying smoked beef-flavoured chips and Coke. He went to sit on a grass bank nearby, smoking a cigarette and enjoying his snack.

Suddenly, unexpectedly, Koen arrived in a car (a 'little Volkswagen') with a woman Sarel had never seen before.

> If I hadn't gone with him, Koen wouldn't have done it. He wanted a little chum [to whom] he could say, 'Look, I can do these things!'

It strikes me, listening to Sarel, that he and Koen were not close friends. Rather, Sarel depicts Koen as a force that, even though Sarel didn't much like him, simply compelled Sarel along – another one of the outside forces driving his narrative.

Koen pulled up alongside Sarel and introduced Marissa to Sarel as Cheryl. He then promptly accused Sarel of stealing from him, saying Amanda had seen him taking a video recorder. He told Sarel to get in the car so they could drive to the beach to talk it through.

Confused by the accusation, Sarel got in the car and Koen drove off. Approaching a more rural area, Koen turned to Marissa and said, 'Hey, lovie, it's time for sex.'

At that moment, it dawned on Sarel what was going on. He hadn't realised why Marissa was in the car. He had presumed she was a friend of Koen's. The reality was a shock.

BH: Did you get a fright?

SV: [Rueful, incredulous] Yes, like any person would get a fright.

Sarel says he was angry at Koen for kidnapping Marissa 'because he suckered me into it; he should have asked'.

Koen parked the car in the bushes near the beach. Still angry at Koen's having lied to him, Sarel got out of the car and walked away, leaving Koen and Marissa alone. He had the knife he'd left the house with tucked into his belt.

Sarel says he didn't see what Koen did. He was sitting a distance away, in front of the car, and just saw heads and arms.

[Quietly] Koen said, 'I've finished having sex with her, and now,' addressing Marissa, 'my friend is here, and you must have sex with him too!' And she said, 'No, I can't have sex with two men in one night.' And it was the way she said it: she looked right in my eyes and said it in a provocative way.

[Loudly, angrily] That's when I got angry. I was already angry with my co-accused. I was already angry with myself for being suckered in this situation, and now I am sitting in this situation not knowing what to do. At the same time, I was sitting with this numb feeling – what the hell is wrong with me? What is going on?

I didn't want to have sex with her. Something set me off. I did it against my will. If she had said nicely, 'Please, no,' I would have said, 'Sweet, fine, man, leave it!' But I was angry at him, and now she makes me even more angry too, so I raped her.

It wasn't actually rape. They say without-permission sex is rape. I didn't have vicious sex with her. It was more like lovemaking, even though it was against her will. It was an intimate thing.

Sarel says that he perceived rape as a violent action against a stranger, tearing her clothes off. 'This rape I did was almost like a date rape,' Sarel clarifies, then incorrectly defines date rape as when a woman has sex then says she didn't want it: 'She didn't struggle at all.' He says that he didn't want to have sex and didn't have an erection, but he raped her nonetheless. 'It wasn't enjoyable, but

I did it anyway,' he says, with a mixture of annoyance and regret, 'to get it finished.'

Sarel's narrative of blaming forces outside himself was the strongest at this moment in this offence. Rather than bear the responsibility for his actions, he gave others control. He was probably tricked into the car, true; but then also it was somehow Marissa's fault for angering him, so, in his internal story, it wasn't really his fault for raping her, and the rape wasn't actually rape. He overlooked the fact that Marissa was taken off the street at knife point and must have feared for her life. This resulted in victim-blaming and minimising the fear and suffering of rape.

Sarel is aware of the contradiction between his actions and his perceptions, though less aware of Marissa's view: alone, with two men, isolated and fearing for her life.

BH: Was she scared?

SV: I don't know; I couldn't say. I really couldn't say. I didn't notice it. I finished, got off, and put the knife on the roof of the car [as it was digging into his hip]. I pulled my trousers back on – I had only taken them off – and smoked a cigarette. That was when my co-accused said, 'What shall we do with her? Should we leave her here? Leave her stark naked and drive away?' That's when I said, 'What would Nick do with her?'

Old Nick, the Devil. Sarel says he wanted to remind Koen of their reason for kidnapping a woman: to pay homage.

The only reason we did this, kidnapped a woman in her car, was for sacrifice. That's where my mind was, to do that. To draw a circle, a pentagram, make fire on the five points, and cut her throat, then drink her blood. In a ritual, a sacrifice ritual. We wanted to do this as a sacrifice, that was the message I wanted to get across to him. That's where my mind was, and then he goes off his head. He decides no, he grabs her by the throat, drags her out the car, grabs a knife and stabs her full of holes, then cuts her throat. That's not how you do it.

Sarel relates this in the annoyed tone of an administrator irritated with a colleague's inability to follow agreed corporate procedure. 'Stupid!' he spits. 'That wasn't a sacrifice!'

Sarel returns to this repeatedly, that this should have been a ritual sacrifice to gain power. He thus places the responsibility for the action firmly with Satanism and, by implication, outside himself. In court, his lawyer described him and Koen as having been motivated to look for a pretty woman to kidnap and kill, then steal her car. 'That wasn't what it was about at all,' objects Sarel. 'He loses his head: stabbed the woman, cut her throat, and the whole thing was a mess.'

He expands, 'I knew I was in trouble afterwards,' describing the transformation in Koen during the crime: muscles tensed, eyes wide, pupils dilated, 'like when you're on pills,' his breath a deep gargle.

'She said, 'Please don't kill me, please don't kill me,' as he strangled her, Sarel tells me. He describes her body spasming and gurgling, then him helping Koen to lift her out of car. 'Is she dead?' he asked. 'Let's see,' said Koen, and took out his penknife and stabbed her with it.

> I didn't feel anything. I took out my knife and, lightly – I didn't want to cut her, I just wanted to show if she had a reaction – I drew the knife across her neck, lightly, and unfortunately it was a bit hard, and broke the skin, made a small cut and some blood came out. This freaked [Koen] out, so he grabbed the knife and cut. He shoved me to one side and went berserk. He was pale, his eyes were round, it didn't look like Koen. It's another person, a thing, it's not Koen.

So, according to Sarel, not only was the true violence committed by someone other than himself, that person was also under the influence of a potent external force: 'He just tore her up and left her, because that's what he wanted, and I couldn't stop him,' Sarel says, then mimics Koen's growling.

> He looked like he was slaughtering a sheep. I got scared. What is he doing now? I wanted to go, and get away. [Nauseated sound] She lay there. And she turned around,

lying on her hands, holding her stomach. I realised she wasn't dead. I threw a cloth over her. My co-accused said, 'She's dead,' and I agreed with him, so that he doesn't go back and hurt her more. My co-accused ... would have ... hurt her. His eyes were wild.

The combined might of Koen and the character of Satanism appears to have overwhelmed Sarel's will. Of course, believing this both justified his actions and reduced any guilt and responsibility he may have had for what had happened. His narrative distanced him, making him a passive onlooker.

He took Marissa's rings and put them on his fingers. He says he had intended to 'give them back'.

When the police got me in the Murder and Robbery [Unit] and asked, 'Where are the rings?' I thought, Oh, shit, they are still on my fingers. Geez, things happened so quick: whip-whip-whip-whip, they happened.

Sarel lapses into a long pause, like when he describes his regret at the end of a relationship.

SV: I went back to the flat. I ran straight to the mirror to look at myself. My pupils, and the coloured part of my eye, the whole thing was black. It gave me a fright. I was also white in the face.

BH: How did you feel?

SV: Cold. I didn't have a sense of what was going on around me. I felt like an animal. I didn't know this world; what must I do here? What's going on here? That's how I felt.

He describes Koen wiping himself off at their flat, throwing away the knife.

Slowly, slowly, it went. He retreated back inside. Until [Koen] says, 'Here's a beer. Sit here, drink a beer.' Then I got into bed and slept. I felt like sleeping.'

Waking the next day, Sarel still felt under the influence of an otherworldly power. He says his 'human understanding' of the environment was gone, and he had to think about everything, like how a traffic light worked or how to cross the road safely, like 'an alien in another world'. These feelings seemed to ebb and flow over the coming days.

He and Koen wandered down to the beach the next day. They lay down on the beach and slept. 'I felt tired, exhausted, like I had no energy.'

Koen apparently wanted to take another woman that day, and he laid out his plans for a series of kidnaps, a daring crime spree, and then escaping.

They were arrested the next day. 'They wouldn't have got us if we had gone out, but Koen said he didn't want to, [he] said he was tired.' Just as Sarel blames Koen for the crimes, he blames him for their capture.

The arresting police announced that the duo were charged for attempted murder. 'Attempted murder? How come "attempted" murder?' Sarel remembers Koen asking. 'Then they said, "The woman is not dead."'

BH: Were you surprised?
SV: No, I wasn't. I saw her turn over. I knew she was alive.

In prison, Sarel suffered more strange phenomena. He felt full of boiling energy, falling asleep and awakening by the basin in his cell with no memory of how he had got there. He reports speaking in strange voices and accents, odd sensations and feelings of pressure within him. He wanted darkness around him and said that this preference for the nocturnal persisted: from the time of his crime, 'I don't feel peaceful in light. During the day, I don't feel human. I feel sleepy. But [in] the night, I'm wide awake.' He can't explain his alert restlessness at night, saying he was scared of the dark as a child, but now 'I would be very happy to live permanently in the dark', 'just wearing black clothes.'

Sarel says he is now a different person from the one he was as a child, implying the lasting effect of satanism and occult influence and saying he wants to be around a fire, dancing and chanting in the night. The malignant cold feeling that filled him during his crime has never come back, though, even when he has tried to attain the same emotion and numbness again. 'It's not there. It's gone.'

He never wanted to kidnap another woman after that, he says.

> It bothers me, these crimes. The thing is, I think back to the crimes a lot. I try to find answers. I ask myself, what happened that night? What the hell happened there? What was wrong with me? I ask myself sometimes: why didn't I walk away? Every time I come back to the conclusion: you were paralysed, you couldn't. It's as if something held you there. [Deeper voice] 'You're not going away from this area. Otherwise, you're going to pay.'

Sarel seems, at first glance, to be an unlucky victim of circumstance. Reeling emotionally from a breakup with a girlfriend, heavily influenced by his interest in the occult, he met the wrong person at precisely the wrong time.

Sarel clearly wanted to kill a woman as a 'sacrifice' to gain occult power. Without his lifelong obsession with the occult, he wouldn't have wanted to kill anyone. Without Koen, it's moot whether he would have done anything towards that 'goal' at all. Sarel said he wanted to sacrifice a woman and Koen seemed to have the energy, the agency, to turn those musings into action.

When Koen took leadership, though, with Sarel in a supporting role, sacrifice seemed to be forgotten. Rape, and sex, came to the fore. Sarel numbly went along with this. It's hard to say precisely why, though Sarel speaks of both he and Koen being transformed by demonic forces. He describes himself as having been swept along by circumstances, complying while cold inside, under the influence of forces that he felt more powerfully than himself.

Sarel's narrative betrays him, however. Blaming a co-defendant who helped encourage and initiate a crime could relieve the moral pressure on Sarel. But, unlike his short friendship with Koen, his dominant internal characters, The Girlfriends and The Occult/ Satanism, did the same thing across his life course. The character of The Girlfriends gave him a sense of belonging and a community. The Occult gave him a similar community – and a means to obtain power over a society by which he felt slighted. This gradually morphed into the more violent form of Satanism as he yearned for more power.

Satanism and The Girlfriends had the same ultimate effect on Sarel: they made him act as if he had no autonomy or will of his own. He was made helpless by this narrative device: pulled across the country, going AWOL from the army for love or sucked downwards into rape and attempted human sacrifice as part of a 'spiritual war'. Whether or not supernatural powers do exist, the belief in a force outside yourself, changing the way you act, is a powerful one.

This is the fifth killer story: relinquishing control by placing power in the characters of other people or in evil human-like external forces; the other, outside. Like a soldier who kills under orders, if you believe someone is directing your actions, then you don't take responsibility for the suffering you cause and you then minimise the suffering of your victims.

PART II
CREATION

6 I am a victim

In August 2019, Nicole Engelbrecht contacted me on Twitter, introduced her podcast, and said she'd stumbled across my PhD during her research. To my surprise, she'd actually read it: my thesis is a solid 629 pages long and academic writing is less than gripping. Yet, luckily, Nicole had been gripped.

It wasn't just flattery that made me agree to appear on her True Crime South Africa podcast. I liked Nicole's focus and her ethics. I'd avoided true crime, disliking the sensationalism, the lazy caricatures of evil monsters and badly lit crime scenes. Yet Nicole spoke about focusing on the victims. She seemed genuinely interested in understanding the reality of crime and respected the ethical guidelines I followed. So in 2020 I appeared on her podcast as 'A South African Mindhunter'. It fed the growing urge I had to tell the story of my conversations with serial murders, to put those narratives to work.

We kept chatting – through the pandemic, online, bouncing ideas back and forth. Then began drafting chapters. Then delving into the stories that didn't make it into my degree work. Then shaping each killer story.

There is a principle in forensic science that states 'every contact leaves a trace'. This, formulated in the 19th century by Dr Edmond

Locard, who became known as the Sherlock Holmes of France, is Locard's exchange principle. It holds that whenever there is contact between two items, there will be an exchange of material. Thus, when a criminal commits a crime, 'wherever he steps, whatever he touches, whatever he leaves, even unconsciously, will serve as a silent witness against him', as noted in Paul Kirk's 1953 book *Crime Investigation*. 'Not only his fingerprints or his footprints, but his hair, the fibres from his clothes, the glass he breaks, the tool mark he leaves, the paint he scratches, the blood or semen he deposits or collects.'

We discovered that a similar phenomenon happens with stories. Digging into other people's stories leaves traces on you. You can't reflect on narrative, the stories humans tell, without reflecting on your own.

Neither Nicole nor I had intended to tell our own stories in this book. We both baulked at the seeming self-importance of it. Weirdly, though, we felt that we were left with little choice: it was the same principle of exchange, except this time we were responding to the shared humanity in the killer stories.

Nicole and I shared our stories in bits and pieces, across video calls and shared documents.

We first got into Nicole's story when we were discussing the darkness of the material in which we have immersed ourselves in our respective careers. As Nicole commented, 'A common question I get in interviews is, "How does this work impact your mental health?" The question is usually delivered with some version of dread-like look on the interviewer's face as they try to imagine sifting through horrendously violent cases, day after day, week after week, pretty much non-stop for five years (so far).'

The first time she was asked this question, she was taken aback. She had never thought about that. It worried her. If all these so-called 'normal people' were telling her that they would be horribly affected by the type of work she does, why wasn't she losing sleep at night like everyone said she should?

'Don't get me wrong, the stories I talk about are horrific,' she says. 'Talking to victims' families is heartbreaking, and every single unsolved case stays with me. There are times when I have to put off certain cases because they are a bit much for the emotional capacity I have that week. But still, I'm not impacted in the negative way people seem to think I should be.'

Nicole had a nagging worry that she was a psychopath. She started calling it 'emotional resilience', telling people it was just a natural thing she was blessed to have. A radio presenter saw straight through that before she did. 'Yeah, maybe one day you'll write a book about how you got that emotional resilience, because I bet it's a story people need to hear,' he quipped.

Nicole laughed and didn't think about that comment again for a long time. Then one day she was listening to a psychology podcast about childhood trauma (a light palate-cleanser from true crime fare, clearly) and the person they were interviewing was talking about 'compartmentalisation'. She'd heard the term from people she'd interviewed who worked in law enforcement, forensic pathology and the like – careers where they were regularly exposed to horrendous things. They had expressed compartmentalisation as the ability to put the horror in a box, along with their human emotions about it, and pack it away on a shelf in their brain so that they could do the job they had come to do.

'Ideally, one should go back regularly to the boxes to unpack them,' Nicole said, 'but that doesn't always happen. I'd figured that compartmentalisation was a skill you learnt out of necessity when you worked in these jobs. Perhaps there was a section in the police training manual called "How to look at murdered children and not cry right away". But the guest on this podcast was using the term in a different context. She explained that compartmentalisation is something that children develop as a coping mechanism when they grow up in chaotic or traumatic environments. I don't have very many "holy shit!" moments, but that was one of them.'

Then Nicole gave me a 'holy shit!' moment of my own. 'I was reading your chapter on Sarel and his description of his dad being a lifelong criminal, and instead of thinking, That's a shame, I thought, Oh, same here.'

Her dad, Nicole explained, was essentially an international drug trafficker. He was arrested when she was 16 years old while trying to smuggle drugs into the United Kingdom, and was convicted. She never saw him again. He had several prior offences in that country (as well as in South Africa) and was given a long sentence. He died in prison in 2018, though she found that out only two years later.

Nicole says that her father's disappearing from her life had never been much of an issue for her because he was a phantom even when he was physically present. 'My mother told me I was better off without him, and I couldn't deny that. One of the few memories I do have of him is him telling me I should study hard because the family needed a good [free] criminal lawyer on call. He wasn't joking.'

Nicole then shared something even more personal. She says that criminality wasn't the only disease that ran through her family – her father 'wasn't the only one with criminal tendencies in my family of birth' – and it wasn't even the most dangerous. Substance-use disorders afflicted most of her family members to some extent, and as a result she had witnessed domestic violence. Also, while she knows for sure about her father's drug and fraud crimes, there were other stories she'd been told, about worse things – 'things that I've never been able to confirm and maybe I don't want to'.

'What I realised through reading your killer stories of the men you interviewed is that there is actually very little, and also just enough, that separates me from these men,' she told me. 'Within the "just enough" are the things that had me end up talking about people in prison instead of being in one, like my dad and these men.'

She sees herself in many of these men's stories, she says – 'The child of a criminal, the child of substance abusers, witnessing domestic violence, and how the stories the adults in my life told themselves got them through the day and kept them trapped.' She said that it was only when she was in her thirties that she really started to understand how that early chaos had shaped who she had become: 'Now I see that there was some X factor that helped me walk a parallel path to a different place than the one these men arrived at.'

Working with me on this project made Nicole analyse many of

the stories she tells herself, about a wide variety of things, daily. 'Perhaps most importantly, it has made me reassess the story of a six-year-old child of substance abusers, domestic violence and criminality, and the person she might be becoming. I wasn't a psychopath after all. I was a six-year-old girl who had learnt how to put things in boxes to survive, and I never lost that skill. Instead, I now use it to be able to tell stories that need to be told.'

Would she be able to do this work if she had never been that six-year-old girl? 'Maybe. Maybe not. But in a probably unhealthy way, I'm grateful for it.'

I'm not sure Nicole's gratitude is unhealthy at all. Another question she is asked frequently in interviews is 'What got you into true crime?' The interview version of the answer is some version of 'I've always been a true crime fan' or 'When I was in Grade 8 my classmate's little sister was murdered' or even simply 'I think South Africa needs a true-crime podcast'. These answers are not entirely a lie, they are just not the complete truth. They are the portion of the story Nicole allowed herself to express.

The process of helping to author this book has allowed her to explore her reasons in more depth, and with more nuance. She's faced up to possibilities she hadn't previously, like 'how close I came to being the subject of a true crime podcast rather than the host of one. Perhaps as a victim, maybe even as a perpetrator.'

I was struck by the image of a very young Nicole, always the observer, quietly on the fringes of the action playing out violently metres away, poised on the edge, ready to become either another victim or another criminal. Instead, this became her superpower. She owned this role, becoming a witness to a nation's trauma through her podcast.

Her past had a purpose, and it bestowed on her the superpower of resilience to see her mission through.

◆

In all these killer stories, we've focused on the contents of the story. Inner characters, for example, are part of these contents. We've seen how important they are in driving the action forward, in the mind of the murderer and in the outside world.

Now we are exploring the overall structure of the plot in the killer stories and the position the storyteller takes in relation to the world. This 'victim' plot structure places the teller at the mercy of the world: he is not an active agent; he is passive, pushed about by circumstance.

Two of the oldest genres in Western literature are those of romance and tragedy. A 'romance', in this historical sense, isn't about romantic love. It's about a person overcoming obstacles. This person shows early promise. Life then challenges them and they fall into crisis, but through the power of their character they rise again to their former (and perhaps even greater) glory. From a high point to a low, then back to a high, this plot line describes the shape of a smile.

A tragic plot line, in contrast, traces a frown. The tragic hero has promise, and they rise in life. However, a fatal flaw in their character conspires with events around them and leads to their downfall. Now split from the rest of the world, the tragic hero remembers their past glory and resigns themselves to their doom. Many of William Shakespeare's most famous plays – *Othello*, *Macbeth*, *Hamlet*, *Romeo and Juliet* – revolve around tragic heroes. Offenders who use a tragic narrative show the same fatalistic acceptance: their crimes were not really 'in their hands' and the chances of anything improving were slim.

We as human beings tend to justify certain types of hate. Of course, we know that hating someone based on their race, appearance and beliefs is ridiculous. The great faiths of the world all encourage us to love our fellow human beings, and to seek to understand those who are different from ourselves. Yet we have designed exceptions to the rule. Some of these exceptions are even dressed up in the clothing of virtue. Perhaps the greatest of these is the exception around revenge.

The storyline around revenge is simple: An innocent person is wronged. They are wronged by someone who is bad. This wronged person, the victim, then seeks vengeance. We lean forward in our seats, thrilled in anticipation, as the victim strives towards this

I AM A VICTIM

goal. When it comes, the victim's revenge is complete, bloody. The person who wronged them is crushed. We sit back with satisfied sighs, content. The victim, we feel, has earned his heroism.

This simple pattern is engrained in the stories of our culture. The Old Testament of the Bible is red with stories of victimised people rising up in revenge, or having their vengeance enacted by the hand of God. Retribution sells, too. Some of the most popular films of recent decades are simple tales of victims taking very violent revenge on their oppressors: the *John Wick* series, the *Jack Reacher* series, the *Kill Bill* films, *The Revenant, Gladiator, Braveheart, The Equalizer* (another series), *Taken* (yet another series) ... the list is long and goes on. The list is even longer if you include movies in which victims humiliate their oppressors more subtly (*Pretty Woman*, anyone?). There is a narrative in our society that associates a sense of closure and pleasure with people who have been wronged seeking revenge. A victim avenging a wrong is accepted.

What, though, if it seems that the world has made you its victim? If the world has treated you badly, you are allowed to lash out in return. Being a victim justifies revenge, not just on one person, but on the whole world.

Revenge stories echo contemporary revenge films, and also find echoes in the city of Liverpool in the United Kingdom, which contains some of the most impoverished neighbourhoods in England.

Many cities in the north of the country suffered in the 1980s as the factories at their industrial hearts stopped beating – and Liverpool suffered as badly as any. Into the gap left by factories and steady employment poured drugs. As a port city, Liverpool was well positioned for the importation of narcotics and firearms from continental Europe. This gave rise to a web of organised crime groups and street gangs and also low-level criminals stealing to feed their status or (more often) their cripplingly expensive drug habits: people trapped by circumstance, association and addiction into a lifestyle of crime.

In 1995 committed academic researcher Shadd Maruna started interviewing ex-prisoners in Liverpool to understand how they

133

'went straight' after a criminal career. In academic parlance, this is called 'desisting'. Initially, he sought ex-prisoners willing to talk, becoming known in ex-offender circles as, in his words, 'the crazy Yank who will pay you to talk about your life.' As more volunteers started finding him (sometimes in the form of late-night phone calls to his home), gradually his one-man mission expanded into a funded research team.

Maruna and his team spoke to people committing property crimes, theft and drugs. He recorded the life stories of 50 offenders, 20 of whom were still actively committing crime and 30 of whom had stopped offending.

The two groups of interviewees were carefully matched. Both groups had grown up in tough neighbourhoods with few opportunities to make a living through legal means. They had experienced physical and emotional abuse; they had struggled with drug and alcohol addiction; and they were extensively involved in crime, usually from a young age. All had poor employment records and had spent significant amounts of time either in prison or being supervised by the criminal justice system.

Maruna's analysis found patterns, and differences, in the narratives told by these two groups. Active offenders, he discovered, tended to characterise themselves as pawns with little or no control over their future. Contrary to popular portrayals, they were not so much committed to a criminal lifestyle as resigned to it. They 'seemed fairly accurate in their assessment of their situation (dire), their chances of achieving success in the "straight" world (minimal), and their place in mainstream society ("need not apply").'

Looking at the unfriendly world around them, they decided that they had nothing left to lose, so they might as well chase happiness through material gain and crime – the 'one big score' that would mean they could live a life of ease.

They blamed their involvement in crime on poverty, peers and social stigma. This narrative gave active offenders a sense of freedom: they no longer had to worry about succeeding. 'Intentionally failing,' comments Maruna, 'may be less stressful on a person's ego than trying to succeed and failing anyway.' Maruna called this narrative of being powerless victims of an inhospitable environment a 'condemnation script'. Unfairly treated by the world, the self-stories of the 20 active Liverpool offenders doom them to deviance.

Gérard Labuschagne is the former head of the SAPS's Investigative Psychology Unit. His doctoral thesis found that many South African serial murderers characteristically feel helpless and inadequate, suggesting that a similar condemnation script may exist for serial murderers. Every killer story in this book shows this to be the case: this condemnation narrative, the belief in being a helpless victim, helps justify each set of crimes. It runs like a dark undercurrent beneath the other narratives.

Look at Jacques. In the first five minutes of our conversation, Jacques had assassinated his parents' characters and their parenting: 'I'm not friends with my parents … [We] never really had a bond.' He dismissed his father as an ineffectual character, falling far short of Jacques' expectations: failing to play with him, or teach him the skills expected of a man, or talk to him, or share personal time. And while his mother 'would make sure I did my homework, and cared for me … there was never really special attention paid, saying, "How can I help you?"' Jacques then segued into describing her as raising him with strict discipline. In Jacques' narrative, he was the helpless victim of cold and emotionless parents, so his cold and emotionless offences in the world became justified.

In Sisanda's story, the victim narrative was so strong that it is hard to disentangle it from his killer story of revenge and victim-blame. His condemnation script takes on a variety of forms. He was condemned by the hostility of his peers, making a 'hobby' of fighting them, and by the violence in the townships that swirled around him. He was trapped by his own reaction to rejection which, he claimed, he was helpless to resist: 'if you made me angry, to me, for that anger to go away, I have to get hold of you. For that anger to go away, I have to do something to you.' Sisanda blamed the person making him angry for the violence he inflicted on them.

Sisanda ultimately portrayed himself as trapped by an unfair world that denied him his dreams – witness his lament when he failed to be accepted as a pastor, that 'there was no one to speak up for me', and his repeated refrain against God: 'I was angry with God. I wanted to be something different, but things didn't go that way.' God had wronged Sisanda, his anger had captured him, and others had victimised him, so violence became the only option.

Michael returned repeatedly to descriptions of himself as an abused and doomed child alone in a hostile world, becoming part of the rhythm of his story. 'I was always hit', 'I was always wrong', 'There was no one I could go to', 'What's life worth if you're a kid and you're attacked and abused?', 'What's life worth for you if you're not trusted?'

In describing the birth of the Monster character, Michael fired blame at God: 'God, why did you throw me away? Why did you split me from my parents? God, why was I brought up like this? God, what aim did you have for me?'

Later in his narrative, he described the bile rising in his throat as he remembered his first wife getting help from the courts when he got nothing in his hour of need. He blamed his wife, and the courts, for his loss of trust in all people.

He went out to murder following an argument with his wife. The internal character of the Monster, Michael outlined, was a way for the aggrieved victim to take revenge on a neglectful God and gain control over a cruel universe: 'I want to show God that I am God.'

Ultimately, Michael's killer story of disintegration evolved to a point where he transmuted his revenge, in his mind, to salvation: 'I'll see kids being abused. I will tell you not to, and you tell me to go away. Later, you will look for your child. You won't find them. I take children to peace.'

Sarel, too, had a condemnation script running through his killer story, of 'the other, outside'. As in the scripts identified in the Liverpool desistance study, Sarel painted himself as pushed out of the social order of his school, a dirty 'boskind'. Powerless in social circles and in his home life with his stepfather, he turned to the occult to give him control. When discussing what tipped him over into committing rape, Sarel directly invoked the condemnation scripts' characteristic blame of the environment: a girlfriend left him, he crashed a car, he had a debt he couldn't pay, there was no one he could speak to about his problems. 'It was because ... they were part of the life and community, and I wanted to hit it back for all the hard times they had given me.'

Sarel finally relinquished responsibility for this revenge to the combined force of Koen and his alleged demon possessor: 'I had no control over my actions, I had no reaction to my actions ... it's as if I was paralysed ... I had tunnel vision.'

Even in Kyle's foggy non-narrative, he sees other people as frequently unjust and wrong-minded, ganging up on him, the innocent. He repeatedly describes this relentless fight against others, and how he is the helpless victim of their shared power.

This 'victim' killer story provides a pattern to a plot that could be lifted out of a revenge film: the abused child lashes out at his oppressors; the rejected boy grows up to take bloody vengeance on the people who hurt him most deeply; a man breaks the shackles of his upbringing to create something remarkable.

However, by interacting with the characters in each story, and the killer stories of loneliness, revenge, disintegration and the other, outside, the plots plunge into darkness. The abused child grows up to leave a trail of dead women and children, hidden in bushes, on careless display in parks and under highways. The rejected boy becomes an enraged abuser of women; he murders again and again and again, until he finds he has gone further than even he can justify. He can never regain the heights he feels he has lost, or the dreams an older brother instilled in him. The claustrophobic constraints of an emotionally chilly upbringing are broken free of, but not in a way that bestows the man with the connection he craves. Instead, he chooses a self-interested adventure. This adventure leads him to become a nightmare, creeping into nighttime bedrooms with a pistol. It leaves him, too, bemused by the fall that puts him in prison, forever lonely, perhaps.

7 Stories from behind bars

The cell block is dark grey stone, wreathed in darkness and shadows, and the imprisoned men in each cell she passes are patently crazy: whispering, screaming, leering. The trainee walks down this grim corridor, shaken by the imprisoned madmen, until the serial killer pans into view. He is lit vividly, poised as a dancer, his eyes fixed on her.

This describes the first meeting between FBI cadet Clarice Starling and Dr Hannibal Lector in the Baltimore Institute for the Criminally Insane in the 1991 movie *Silence of the Lambs*. It set the tone for much subsequent serial-murder fiction.

My experience of interviewing prisoners behind bars wasn't like this. Real life was – is – different.

The prisons I visited when I spoke to serial murderers were not the dark stone dungeons of cinematic imagination. For the most part, the most vivid impression they left was the vague institutional shabbiness of ageing public buildings the world over. Anyone who grew up in apartheid-era South Africa would be familiar with the polished floors, green/brown paint and thick brick walls, themes in the architecture of our youth, except that the security gates were much bigger and thicker in prisons than in the schools we attended.

With a few notable exceptions, when I interviewed a serial murderer, we sat across a small veneer-topped table loaded with my notepaper, interview schedule and tape recorder, or on chairs facing each other. We were as close as people meeting for a coffee in normal life. We shared coffees in prison, too, brought by either a warder in brown uniform or a prisoner in green. The taste of instant prison coffee, very milky, very sweet, remains a vivid memory. Even more vivid is the smell of prison: a pervasive combination of cheap rolling tobacco and the faint whiff of old sweat in badly washed clothes. A sniff of these odours transports me instantly back to interviews in prisons, with the low autumn sunshine slanting into the room.

There was one prison, though, that was different from the others. I learnt a lesson about humanity there. It was an ultra-maximum-security prison, one closer to the clichés of Hollywood.

A blond warder welcomed me, checking my documents and equipment, and making sure I understood the rules. Next to him on the desk was a riot shield, a thick metal band running around its edge.

'Is this okay?' he asked, pointing to my tape recorder.

'Ja,' I said. 'I have permission.' I showed him the Correctional Services letter.

Inside this prison, the walls were all white. The doors were thicker, inches of steel, and the ceiling was lower, a metal grid. Bulletproof glass was a popular feature.

Here, even the prisoners wore different clothes. Gone were the green fatigues of all the other prisons; here, they wore bright orange. They were not allowed out of their cells without chains around their ankles; some were handcuffed, too, hands cranked up high behind their back. It was an atmosphere designed, I thought, to make you nervous.

I asked to use the toilet before interviewing and was shown an entirely empty tiled room with a single toilet in the one corner. There was an observation strip of thick bulletproof glass opposite. Standing at that lonesome toilet, I found myself running my brain through all the prison movies I had seen, keeping one eye on the door behind me, thinking that, trapped in here with one of the residents, I'd be squashed like an ant. It was too easy to imagine an orange-suited figure appearing in the doorway, my head being smashed into unyielding tiles.

In the interview room, there was a metal-rimmed table bolted to the floor. I had a chair. On the opposite side of the table was a stool; this, too, was bolted to the floor. There were two iron rungs on its legs.

On this day, I was meeting Theo. I had seen the press photographs of him when he had been arrested: he was a big man then, broad and strong. One of his victims had been so badly beaten that the cause of death was suffocation caused by the bones of her broken mouth slipping down her throat. So I was nervous.

Then Theo walked in. Prison seemed to have withered him. He peered at me from behind the thick-rimmed government-issue glasses that would be fashionable three decades later. His hands were still big, though: a legacy of the man he had been.

His ankles were chained, his hands up high behind his back, forcing him to bend slightly forward. The warders shuffled him around the desk and sat him down on the stool, looping the chains at his ankles around the iron loops in his chair. (Oh, so that's what they're for, I thought.) My nervousness grew.

Theo settled onto the stool as they unbolted his handcuffs. As soon as his hands came free, he sprang up and shot one towards me.

I flinched back, then realised: he was just wanting to shake hands.

Well, that was uncool, said the voice in my head, as I shook his hand. Theo didn't seem to notice.

Theo spoke for the next eight-and-a-half hours.

I had been expecting the violent intimidator of my imagination, but what I got was a human being who just wanted to talk freely to someone. That was my lesson in humanity in the ultra-maximum-security prison: whoever we are, whatever we've done, we all want to tell our stories to a sympathetic ear, without judgement. We all want to be heard.

Looking back, it's not surprising. Research has shown again and again the effect stories have on us. Listening to a moving narrative evokes a range of brain chemicals: dopamine to satisfy us, oxytocin to build social relationships, adrenalin to excite. Stories create emotions and emotions influence us.

What is a story, though? How and why does our brain create them? An elegant experiment tells us.

This experiment took place in 1944, in the United States, during the final days of the Second World War. It involved 114 university undergraduates. It's not uncommon for researchers to use undergraduates in their experiments: undergraduates are the one group of people that universities have a lot of, and who researchers can access pretty much any time they need. It's less usual for all the research subjects to be women, but at the time this experiment took place, the young men who would normally be found at university were, presumably, scattered across the last battlefields of Africa, Asia and Europe.

The experiment was run by two researchers. Fritz Heider, 48 years old, had worn glasses since his eyes were injured as a child in Austria. Marianne Simmel, just 21, had fled Nazi Germany as a refugee. Both Heider and Simmel were Jewish, so to stay in their homeland would have meant persecution, even death. They had made America their home and were forging their reputations in the still young field of psychology.

Heider and Simmel showed all the research subjects a short movie. You can still see the film online: the experiment made it famous, even though it is only a minute-and-a-half long and the only action consists of geometrical shapes – a large triangle, a small triangle and a circle – moving silently around a big, empty rectangle.

The research subjects were divided into three groups and each group was given a different set of instructions before and after they watched the film. Dividing research subjects into groups and then testing them separately, is standard experimental practice. It's done to make sure that the results of the experiment are not simply down to chance.

When Heider and Simmel asked the research subjects what they had seen, the results were remarkable.

Only three of the 114 people described exactly what was shown in the film: geometric shapes. Here is one of those three people's description:

> A large solid triangle is shown entering a rectangle. It
> enters and comes out of this rectangle, and each time the
> corner and one half of one of the sides of the rectangle
> form an opening. Then another, smaller triangle and a circle
> appear on the scene. The circle enters the rectangle while
> the larger triangle is within. The two move about in circular
> motion, and then the circle goes out of the opening and
> joins the smaller triangle, which has been moving around
> outside the rectangle. Then the smaller triangle and the
> circle move about together, and when the larger triangle
> comes out of the rectangle and approaches them, they
> move rapidly in a circle around the rectangle and disappear.
> The larger triangle, now alone, moves about the opening
> of the rectangle and finally goes through the opening to
> the inside. It moves rapidly within and, finding no opening,
> breaks through the sides and disappears.

All the other 111 research subjects described the geometric shapes as living beings, humans, animals, birds. These shapes were bound together in dynamic interactions. Here is the description of one of those 111 other research subjects:

> A man has planned to meet a girl and the girl comes along
> with another man. The first man tells the second to go; the
> second tells the first to go, and he shakes his head. Then
> the two men have a fight, and the girl starts to go into the
> room to get out of the way ... She apparently does not want
> to be with the first man. The first man follows her into the
> room after having left the second in a rather weakened
> condition leaning on the wall outside the room. The girl
> gets worried and races from one corner to the other in the
> far part of the room. Man number one, after being silent for
> a while, makes several approaches at her; but she gets to
> the corner across from the door just as man number two
> is trying to open it. He evidently got banged around and
> is still weak from his efforts to open the door. The girl gets

out of the room in a sudden dash just as man number two gets the door open. The two chase around the outside of the room together, followed by man number one. But they finally elude him and get away. The first man goes back and tries to open the door, but he is so blinded by rage and frustration that he cannot open it. So he butts it open and in a really mad dash around the room he breaks in first one wall and then another.

This research has been repeated again and again over the intervening 80 years, with similar results each time. The vast majority of people don't just see geometric shapes changing coordinates. They see fights, chases, love stories and escapes, played out by active, living creatures.

This experiment demonstrates powerfully that we use stories to fill a potentially meaningless world with meaning. At the simplest level, stories do this by linking events together using cause and effect when one or more things happen because of something else: first one thing happens; then this thing causes another thing to happen; and then, because these things happened, a third thing comes to pass. Bingo! A story!

The Pixar movie studio uses a variation of this structure as a spine for its films: 'Once upon a time there was —. Every day, —. One day, —. Because of that, —. Because of that, —. Until finally —. And ever since that day —.' Apply this structure next time you watch a Pixar movie. It's very satisfying watching the structure click into place. Whether it's *Toy Story*, *Finding Nemo* or *Up*, all use the same basic structure of cause and effect.

Heider and Simmel's experiment points to something deeper, though: the fact that our minds impose this order on events without our even realising it. Our brains don't just create cause and effect; our brains' narratives impose motives on the world even when none exists. To our brains, the events in the world don't just happen: they are caused by something. We ascribe inner motivations to inanimate objects ('my computer hates me') or to the weather ('those clouds are angry'). These motives and causes are often framed as social relationships. Thus, in Heider and Simmel's experiment, instead of random shapes, we see 'a man has planned to meet a girl and the girl comes along with another man ...'. Those social relationships, real or not, help to create the stories we tell ourselves about the world. Stories mean that the events of our life didn't just happen: they happened for a reason, caused by something or, more usually, someone.

How can these stories go wrong – so wrong that they could justify the murder of another human being? These are the 'killer stories', when the inner myths we use to make the world meaningful lead to our destruction.

8 The elephant: How we truly make decisions

We think we know why we act the way we do. In truth, we don't.

This is one of the fundamental truths of psychology. From Freud right up to the cutting edge of modern neuropsychology, this is true.

Psychology is a broad field: it encompasses everyone from neurologists measuring minute electrical impulses in human brains, to research psychologists creating vast mathematical models, to counsellors treating the ill, and to academic psychologists shaping philosophies of meaning. All of them share this common understanding: what we observe on the surface of our own minds, the parts we are aware of as we go about our daily business, are not the only parts of our minds that exist. They are not what truly drives many of our actions.

What not many people know about psychology is that there is not just one school of psychology. Not all psychologists agree on what makes a person a person, and why people do the things they do. If you had to go back a century or two, psychology would have seemed a little bit like Hogwarts. You have different houses, or 'schools': instead of Slytherin, Gryffindor, Hufflepuff and Ravenclaw, you'd have the Functionalists, the Structuralists, the

Psychoanalysts, the Gestalt Psychologists and the young upstart Behaviourists.

All of them would be (metaphorically) wearing different-coloured robes and (literally) believing that different things are the most important element in determining human nature. For example, the behaviourists would believe that the best way to understand human nature is through experiments exploring how we behave, and that all human beings are shaped by a pattern of stimulus and response. By contrast, those who believe in psychoanalysis would contend that everything comes back to our childhood experiences and the vast pool of emotions and urges buried out of sight in our unconscious. So the various schools would disagree not just on human nature, but even on what is real and what isn't.

If you read books or articles on the psychology of serial murder, you'll notice that different authors emphasise different aspects of a serial murderer's behaviour and say 'these are the most important ones'. So, for example, a psychoanalytical author in the tradition of Sigmund Freud would write about early-childhood trauma, while a behaviourist would write about the patterns of response that have been built up over your life, their lives. It's not that one author is right and the other is wrong; they just emphasise different things.

Having said that, all schools of psychology would agree on one thing: we think we know why we act the way we do, but we don't.

A great image for understanding our minds is the mahout and the elephant. A mahout is the person who sits on top of an Indian elephant. You've probably seen pictures of them – skinny jockeys perched just behind the elephant's vast head, with their legs tucked beneath them, swaying with the motion of the elephant as it saunters along a jungle path somewhere on the subcontinent. The mahout prods the elephant along, tells it what to do and keeps it on the path.

This mahout is like the conscious, rational part of us, the part that likes facts, figures and logic. An average human male, he weighs about 70 kilograms.

The average Indian elephant weighs 5 400 kilograms. They roll logs out of the way with their trunks, casually shoulder aside trees and effortlessly flatten unwary tourists.

Now, imagine that our elephant spies, through the jungle leaves, an especially juicy bunch of bananas. This particular elephant loves nothing more than bananas, and it is going to charge and get those bananas. Do you think our tiny mahout could control the elephant? Could the mahout stop it crashing through the jungle after its bananas, disregarding the tiny shouting thing on its back?

The elephant is like our unconscious mind. This part of our mind is ruled by symbols and emotions. It is filled with meaning, using all sorts of useful mental shortcuts and biases to help us understand the world. It holds the real power.

Most of the time, the mahout and the elephant work together very well to keep us bumping along with society. When they get out of balance, though, the elephant is the one that psychology wants to influence.

With the growth of advanced brain-scanning technology, we are better able to prove scientifically that we are influenced by things our conscious mind does not fully grasp. The idea that we make decisions based on our emotions, and then apply logic to rationalise the decisions we have made subconsciously, is no longer an idea limited to a psychoanalyst's couch. It has become a scientific fact.

For example, researchers at the University of Southern California used magnetic resonance imaging (MRI) scanners to show that we respond to challenges to our beliefs using the same emotional parts of our brain that are activated when we are physically attacked (as documented in a study by Jonas Kaplan, Sarah Gimbel and Sam Harris). This happens automatically, faster than conscious thought. And another study, with Kaplan as lead researcher, found that the same networks in the brain that were activated when our beliefs were challenged kicked in when people read stories that appealed to their strongly held core values.

Imagine listening to your favourite podcast (maybe even your favourite true-crime podcast). You are sitting quietly at home, unwinding. You are immersed in the story. The host is weaving pictures in your mind with her words. You are transported by her: you are standing beside her as you view the body of the victim. You leap inside the mind of the victim in her last moments, then into that of the murderer as he runs from the scene. Then you are feeling the anguished, helpless grief of the victim's family as they come to terms with their irretrievably changed world.

Scientists who've measured the brain activity of people listening to stories found that it wasn't just the 'listening' parts of the brain that lit up when they heard a good story. Emotions are leaping into being, summoned by the storyteller's words. This isn't an illusion or a fantasy. This reflects actual, measurable brain activity.

Professor Lisa Feldman Barrett from Northeastern University, Massachusetts, runs research that demonstrates the power of words. Her research participants lie in a brain scanner and listen to audio recordings of different situations, each designed to evoke emotions: from waking up to a love note to coming back to your childhood home and being enveloped in hugs. The researchers noticed that the parts of the brain that control our bodily budget – our metabolism, immune system, heart rate and breathing – respond to the language in the stories. As Feldman Barrett says, 'Words have power over your biology – your brain wiring guarantees it.'

Her experiments also found that, even lying still, with eyes closed, the participants' brains showed activity in the regions involved in vision and movement. Their brains were filling in the gaps, transforming a few seconds of audio into sight, motion and emotion.

Scientists at Princeton University went a step further and measured brain activity in people listening to unrehearsed stories, including stories about their first year of high school. As the speakers told their stories about those nervy, exciting life events, the audience's brain activity started to mirror that of the storytellers. As they spoke about their emotions, the scientists saw those emotions in the brains of people listening to them.

Even more powerful, the audience's brains started showing emotions before the story told them to: the audience was anticipating what would come next, and their brains were responding accordingly. In their study, published in the journal of the National Academy of Sciences, the scientists concluded that 'ongoing dynamic interaction between two brains during the course of natural communication revealed a surprisingly widespread neural coupling'. What a vivid term: 'neural coupling' – as if our brains are intertwined invisibly across space and time by threads of emotion and action.

When we tell a story, we are changing the neural activity of the listener. We are making their brain match ours, so they can see what we saw, feel what we felt, for as long as the story lasts.

This body of research shows us how and why stories affect us so powerfully. And if this is how our stories can affect someone else, imagine how your own story shapes your internal world.

We know that human beings create stories to explain their world. Our neurological netherworlds show us that stories trigger our emotions. Emotions trigger actions, then actions become stories.

This loop can happen without our being fully aware of it, in the space between our consciousness and our unconscious. Sometimes, though, this loop can betray us.

9 Nature, nurture, narrative

You may have read the killer stories in this book with a nagging sense of doubt. You may have been thinking, These guys are obviously just plain crazy. These characters have nothing to do with the killers' choices. It's something else. You might think it's because they were abused. For the ones who weren't obviously abused, it's because they were insane. If neither abused nor insane, they are just plain bad people.

By thinking along these lines, you're following in the worthy footsteps of many other enquirers into human nature and behaviour: Why do we think and act as we do? What truly drives people? As we've seen, the different schools of psychology answer this question slightly differently. Each has its own theories about how the human mind works and how it organises the world. Let's illuminate this with a few of the explanations offered for serial murder.

As mentioned in the last chapter, a psychoanalytical practitioner would write about early-childhood trauma, in the tradition of Freud: they would show how the events of the serial murderers' earliest childhood created the template for their lives. A behaviourist would emphasise responses that have built up over the course of their lives: they would note how the environment shaped and encouraged the serial murderers' actions. A modern psychiatrist would search for evidence of mental illness, finding the set of diagnostic labels that would best reflect the serial murderers' mindset. And so on through all the schools of psychology.

The problem is, no single factor can be shown as the cause of serial murder. This is because if you emphasise, for example, the role of childhood abuse in shaping a serial murderer, then you must deal with the awkward fact that for every abused child who becomes a murderer, there are thousands of abused children who do not. In the same vein, while a person with psychosis may kill due to their loss of contact with reality, it's far more likely that they would harm themselves or be harmed by others. For every psychopath in a prison cell, there are probably many more in the world's militaries, businesses, hospitals and governments. For every set of life experiences affecting a serial murderer, you'll find a different set of factors in the life stories of other murderers.

It is perhaps because of this complexity that the most often used definition of serial murder is one that doesn't make any assumptions about what caused the offences. This broad definition, derived from the original Federal Bureau of Investigation research in this field, states that serial murder is two or more separate acts of murder, occurring at different times, in separate events, committed by an individual acting alone or with another.

My Master's thesis illustrates the challenge of such a broad definition. The thesis explored the offence behaviours of the various serial murderers I spoke to. It analysed these behaviours statistically to see what patterns might emerge. These patterns, I figured, would support future investigation.

If all these South African serial murderers did similar things when they committed their crimes, then I'd have expected to see all their behaviours clustering together on the statistical output. This didn't quite happen. The only common factor I found was 'act-focused murder', that is, the serial murderer obviously and clearly meant to kill his victim. The other behaviours were spread across the statistical chart.

This led me to wonder whether the definition of a serial murderer was accurate, or even helpful in understanding crime. Maybe categorising someone as a serial murderer was less important than investigating their criminal journey, that is, their life story: how their criminality developed and how different individuals arrived at the same deadly destination. So I travelled onwards into my doctoral studies and deeper into narrative psychology.

Dr Dan P McAdams' research into narrative psychology guided my emerging ideas 20 years ago, particularly around inner characters and the role they play in our stories. Today, his 200 or more publications explore narrative and the way in which it helps to create our personalities.

The first of these is his 'triadic theory of personality'. I like this theory because it tries to bring together different schools of psychology in a holistic way. I like it even more because it simultaneously illuminates the forces that shape our personalities and demonstrates how complex the reality of human behaviour is.

McAdams proposes three interrelated layers of personality: dispositional traits, characteristic adaptations and life narratives.

Dispositional traits represent the most stable and enduring aspects of our personality, our general behaviour and attributes. By the time we are adults, we have developed consistent patterns of behaviour, emotion and cognition. These explain why people's behaviours, thoughts and feelings are broadly consistent across situations and over time. These traits are what are measured by personality tests, such as the commonly known Myers-Briggs Type Indicator. These traits describe factors such as extraversion (how expressive and outgoing a person is), conscientiousness (how organised and persistent someone is) and neuroticism (how emotionally stable or prone to anxious feelings someone is), to name a few. There are no 'right' or 'wrong' personality traits. They simply describe our internal and enduring characteristics.

Characteristic adaptations describe how we have responded to our external environment. This recognises that we all respond to different stresses, concerns, goals and values, which are in turn influenced by the demands of time, place and social role. So, for example, a person who has a personality high in extroversion, neuroticism and conscientiousness will develop very different characteristic adaptations depending on whether they were born in South Africa in 1980, in South Korea in 1949 or in South Carolina in 2020. The adaptations will, of course, also change according to whether they were born to a rich family or a poor one, whether they were educated or not, what the expectations of society were for someone like them, and so on.

Unlike dispositional traits, characteristic adaptations are more malleable and context-dependent, allowing individuals to adjust their behaviour based on situational demands. These adaptations provide insight into an individual's unique psychological makeup and the strategies they employ to achieve their goals.

McAdams explains on Monmouth College's YouTube channel that much of our lives is lived on the border between turbulence and order. Imagine two people, both born in South Africa in 1980, from the same ethnic group and with similar levels of education. They have similar dispositional traits. Imagine both growing up during the end of apartheid. They have similar values and characteristic adaptations. Both walk to school every day. One day, on the way to school, the first child is hit by a car and crippled. The very same day, just up the same road, the second child is noticed by a talent scout and whisked away to New York to become a fashion model. Totally random things happened to similar people, setting their lives on utterly different paths.

Life stories form the third level of McAdams's model of the personality. Stories, McAdams says, are how we make order out of the random turbulence of our lives: 'things happen in our lives that we don't predict and sometimes they're great, and sometimes they're terrible, and sometimes it's hard to know which; but they don't really follow a pattern because, let's face it, life is pretty random. But we need to make order of it. We need to write it out in our heads, make a story. So the story is neat and clean, and life is dirty and crazy, and all mixed up, and we sort of live on the border between what's happening in our world and the story we're creating.'

◆

Since his first published research in 1980, McAdams has sought to develop our understanding of the roles stories play in shaping our personalities, he and his students have interviewed thousands of Americans, young and old, of all races. Some interviews were face-to-face conversations while other people responded through various forms of survey.

McAdams was looking to identify patterns in the narratives with the level of reliability and validity needed in academic research. Each interview response was analysed using a coding and classification system. These coded interviews were then statistically analysed and, eventually, captured in a steady stream of research papers through the 1980s and 1990s. These papers were broadly concerned with the healthy and positive roles individuals' stories could play.

My journey into narrative came from the opposite direction, looking at the darker and unhealthy stories men tell. I was only just starting on my journey into research when, in April 2001, McAdams and some colleagues published a paper about 'redemption' and 'contamination' in life narratives and their relation to psychosocial adaptation. (Redemption narratives, McAdams later said, 'are my best discovery.)

Put simply, in a contamination sequence, an episode starts well but ends badly. For example, a happy new relationship sours; or a bright student goes on to struggle in the working world. Redemption sequences describe the opposite pattern: a negative beginning becomes a positive ending. More significantly, redemption sequences show people overcoming their negative circumstances or past mistakes to become better versions of themselves.

In his 2001 research, McAdams and his team asked adults aged 35 to 65 and undergraduate students to provide accounts of meaningful episodes in their lives: their earliest memories, the high and low points, those moments where things turned around. The accounts were separated into those containing redemptive and those containating imagery.

The respondents then undertook a series of tests that scored them for generativity, a psychological shorthand term for whether a person is concerned about guiding the next generation, and general levels of psychological wellbeing.

Now comes the cool bit: McAdams matched the two sets of results and made a series of discoveries. First, midlife adults who reported more contamination sequences also reported lower levels of psychological wellbeing. Next, midlife adults who scored high on measures of generativity showed significantly higher levels of redemption and lower levels of contamination sequences. Finally, both young and older people who reported more redemption sequences had higher levels of wellbeing. Even if a person told a story filled with happy content and imagery, the person who included more redemption sequences scored more highly on measures of wellbeing.

These findings showed that not only can contamination sequences make you feel worse, but redemption narratives can make you happier, no matter your age; and as you get older, they can predict how much you care about the next generation. This simple story-telling device, McAdams showed, can change your outlook on your life and the lives that follow yours.

Just as with victim narratives, we build these redemption narratives by drawing on the stories that exist in the culture around us. Remember, though, that redemption narratives don't deliver the simplistic message of 'life is always good'. They invite us to acknowledge that things were bad or that we made things worse for ourselves, but then overcame them and made our lives better.

I admit that McAdams's findings seemed quite far from the experience of the men I spoke to. In every case, the men I spoke to showed the opposite: all their stories contained condemnation scripts, giving form to the idea that the world was an unkind place and that they were helpless within it.

The parallels with McAdams's contamination sequences are clear, however: all the men I interviewed showed the shape of a tragedy, that is, a swift and terrible decline, doomed to end badly. This is not surprising. After all, I was speaking to these men at a low point in their lives. Many had not been imprisoned long, so, you could reason, they were at the lowest point in their story, the nadir, as they faced years of imprisonment and regret.

All the same, I felt a niggle of doubt that anyone who had committed crimes as serious as those perpetrated by the men I spoke to could redeem themselves or change their narratives. McAdams was interviewing free and healthy people and he mentioned that many possessed the belief from their early years that they were worth something and destined for better things. This was certainly not the case with the people I spoke to: they had endured years of shame, neglect and abuse. None had left childhood with the sense he was a worthy and valued human being. All had committed the worst possible acts on other human beings. Maybe they were doomed.

◆

We've already seen that stories are powerful and affect us at a neurological level. They can trigger emotions, influencing the way we think and feel, all without our knowing it. This insight takes us deeper: our internal story helps us organise our experiences. Rather than seeing randomness everywhere, a story helps us make sense of our experiences, and so maintain our reality. The undergraduates in Fritz Heider and Marianne Simmel's film experiment didn't see random chaos: they saw connection, motives and stories. Jacques', Sisanda's and Michael's stories didn't describe them randomly drifting through life and accidentally killing a few people on the way, for instance: they had purpose and direction, and formed a whole. And none of the killers made it their 'life mission' – the aim of their story – to kill people; rather, the killing happened as a side-effect of their killer stories.

Life narratives are thus the autobiographical stories that individuals construct to give their lives meaning and coherence. They reflect the individual's identity and how they make sense of their past, present and future. As you've seen in the killer stories we've discussed so far, they include key life events, turning points, themes and self-defining memories that contribute to an individual's understanding of who they are and their place in the world. They shape not only how individuals perceive themselves but also how they relate to others and broader society.

A narrative explanation does not depend on any features in the person's life, their traits or adaptations, or the random events that befall them. Rather, our life narratives integrate all these events, dispositional traits and characteristic adaptations into the familiar cause and effect of a story. Stories weave together 'nature' and 'nurture'.

Just as we become the authors of our stories, so our stories change how we live our lives. We are continually moulded throughout our lives by our own idea of ourselves. Our selves – our sense of who we are in the world – are being shaped by the secret engines of our stories.

So how are these secret self-making stories shaped? Narrative psychology outlines that we human beings, our behaviour and who we think we are are socially constructed. The internal stories that help us make sense of our lives are not just dreamed up in the private darkness of our skull. Our stories are shaped in dialogue with the world around us and our interactions with others influences the way we experience reality. Our story, and thus our reality, is constructed through conversation and social interactions.

Most simply, by picking events that match our existing perceptions, we 'layer up' our stories of our selves. As these grow, we pay less attention to things that don't fit our stories – and more attention to the things that do. Thus our stories can become self-reinforcing. This is why some of our killers seem to have such a narrow view of who they are and their options in life. They simply don't see a different way of tackling the problems their lives have thrown at them.

When you first hear it, the idea that our stories, and our sense of who we are, are socially constructed can sound rather abstract and philosophical. However, many South Africans cherish this belief when they celebrate ubuntu. The Xhosa proverb describes ubuntu as 'a person is a person through other persons'; or, as Archbishop Desmond Tutu poetically described it, 'My humanity is caught up, is inextricably bound up, in yours.' Look at Sisanda's story, for example. All the characters that led him deeper into violence and death were born out of the social interactions around him.

Our stories are created not just by direct relationships, however. They are also shaped by wider society and the stories commonly told in that society.

Over the years, people who study stories have found many ways to structure our stories, their common patterns, topics and contents. Among the best known of these is Joseph Campbell's 'The Hero's Journey'.

Campbell, an academic researcher of comparative religion, had a career spanning the middle part of the 20th century. He collected, analysed and compared ancient mythologies and classical stories from all over the world. He started finding common patterns that spanned continents and cultures. Similar characters, gods, problems and victories emerged in different cultures at different times, Campbell found, pointing towards a common human experience. Like the Pixar movie-plot structure mentioned earlier, many stories followed a pattern he labelled 'The Hero's Journey'. A hero is called to adventure, leaves his or her ordinary world behind, finds a mentor, faces a trial, and then returns armed with new knowledge to face a final challenge that will allow the hero to rejoin his or her community. It has been seen as a universal template for the human experience of growth, self-discovery and the trials we face, and has been noted in stories as diverse as *The Odyssey* and *Lord of the the Rings*. It has also been cited as inspiration to a myriad storytellers, most famously George Lucas, the creator of *Star Wars*.

Of course, 'The Hero's Journey' shares problems with many models claiming to have found universal truths. It was identified by a white man, studying the world from a Western perspective, and can be seen as insensitive to the full range of mythological and storytelling traditions. While some of Campbell's statements about mythologies don't chime with someone growing up in an African context and 'The Hero's Journey' is simply another way we can shape a story we tell, I think it has relevance in our contemporary world, buzzing with a wider range of competing and complex stories. This relevance springs from Campbell's insistence that ancient myths should not be seen as just dusty relics, lying irrelevantly in old books. Rather, he says, they should be seen as powerful tools which affect us now in our day-to-day lives.

These societal myths can be expressed in many ways in our culture: in music, books, films and conversation. The myths are constantly being revised and updated – just look at the new range of imaginary heroes springing out of the Marvel cinematic universe, replacing the old Greek gods as reference points for our culture. These modern myths inform and inspire us, giving us ways to shape our own internal narratives.

Criminals use these stories from our wider culture too in order to create their own myth and boost their power.

◆

Roberto Saviano has spent the best part of two decades in hiding. He has round-the-clock police protection, moving from house to house and town to town with the intentional erratic randomness of someone who knows that any habitual pattern, any consistency, could bring on a sudden violent death.

Saviano's crime? He wrote a book.

Gomorrah, first published in Italy in 2006, feels as if it was written in a fit of rage. Saviano's outrage was directed at the Italian mafia families, the Camorra, which he saw infiltrating and infecting every aspect of the Neapolitan society in which he grew up. Saviano lived within, watched and studied every aspect of the Camorra's influence. He worked in the quasi-illegal industries they fed. He tracked the misery the mafia families caused to the people they employed. He raced on his Vespa from mob execution to mafia shooting. He noticed the nameless immigrants who died unknown and were buried in unmarked graves, and spoke to kids in the urban slums who were becoming the drug runners and foot soldiers for powerful clans. Saviano was frustrated by their short lives and quick deaths in the service of the rich people who fed off them.

He saw the power the Camorra mafioso wielded, be it economically through their businesses, politically through their contacts and wealth or psychologically through the power they exerted over the minds of people. This psychological power, Saviano argued, was fuelled by the stories they shaped and the images they created of the gangster lifestyle.

In one striking passage in his book, Saviano described sneaking into the abandoned mansion of a mafia boss. The mansion had been hidden away behind high walls in the heart of a rundown part of Naples. It was a grandiose statement of power, trashed and left to rot after the owner's downfall at the hands of Italian prosecutors.

Local urban myth had it that this villa, dubbed 'Hollywood', had been modelled on the villa from the 1983 movie *Scarface* which follows the rise and fall of the fictional Cuban Miami gangster Tony Montana. It's a heady tale of extreme wealth and power, ending with Montana dying, machine gun in hand, in a hail of bullets on the balcony of his glorious mansion. The local mafia boss had reportedly wanted to tap into the myth's power and so he commissioned architects and builders to create a slice of Hollywood in the middle of a downtrodden Naples neighbourhood. The rumours of the Hollywood mansion rising right off the silver screen behind the high concrete walls just added to the mafioso's mystique in the neighbourhood.

Saviano slipped into the grounds to see if the rumours were true and he found the mansion to be everything the legend had promised. Doric columns mimicking those of ancient Greece and Rome created an awe-inspiring facade. In the entrance hall, two enormous marble staircases soared up to a second-floor balcony. An office opened out onto the balcony, just as in *Scarface*.

Amid the ostentatious architecture, Saviano reflected on how much of the mafia's imagery was borrowed from Hollywood. Mafia bosses, he said, no longer carried knives and worked their way up from the street; rather, they went to good schools and graduated, travelled the world, watched movies and TV, and then took their place in what Saviano called 'the offices of the mechanism of power'. 'It's not the movie world that scans the criminal world for the most interesting behaviour. The exact opposite is true,' Saviano noted. He then listed examples of this theft from societal myths: the term 'godfather' wasn't used by Italian-American gangsters until after the movie of the same name was released in 1972; a rising young mafioso modelled his look after that of the anti-hero star of the 1994 movie, *The Crow*; and female bodyguards dressed like Uma Thurman in the 2003 movie *Kill Bill*; while hitmen mimicked the sideways pistol-shooting of a Tarantino film and so injured rather than killed their targets. This is a perfect example of a cultural narrative being used to inform an individual story.

Saviano's insights removed the mafia from the pedestal their myths had built for them. At best, a mafia bosses became no better than the rest of us, borrowing stories to patch together their image of themselves. At worst, they became slightly ridiculous pretenders, emperors without any clothes.

◆

Nowadays, the debate about nature versus nurture seems old-fashioned, and the split between psychological schools is less extreme than it once was. It's no longer a question of whether we human beings are born a certain way or are made that way by our environment. Rather, we now acknowledge the complex interplay between nature and nurture in shaping who we are.

Finding a single reason why some people become serial murderers is elusive, because there are seldom single reasons why we human beings become anything. Rather, we are the result of the complex interconnectedness of the various parts of our personalities and our wider environment. We are each an unpredictable blend of similar and unique. Our personalities are an evolving and dynamic system, incorporating both stability and change, a combination of dispositional traits, characteristic adaptations and our life narratives. Any catastrophic event, serial murder included, is the result of multiple causes, influences and random events.

Our life narratives are a way we make our lives meaningful and coherent. We shape these narratives by drawing on our experiences, our relationships and the stories that are woven through our culture. This is true for you or me, as much as for an Italian mafia boss or for a serial murderer.

The killer stories we have explored so far all represent these men's ways of dealing with the world. Kyle's fog, Jacques' story of loneliness, Sarel's surrender to forces outside himself, Sisanda's tale of revenge richly earned and Michael's coping with trauma by fracturing his inner characters: these are all ways of managing the world. All became their truth.

There are patterns in our narratives, things that can lift us up or lead us astray. We can change these patterns.

10 New origins

Stars are symbols of permanence. Human myths put immortal gods and warriors and creatures in their unchanging lights. Wheeling in their set patterns, centuries of travellers have navigated by the constellations.

As a child, I learnt the basics of navigating by the stars. One of the most distinctive constellations is Orion the hunter. Orion strides the heavens, weapon dangling from his belt, arm raised, flanked by his hunting dogs, facing off against the galactic bull, Taurus, or chasing the sisters marked by the Pleiades star cluster. I was taught to find the three bright stars that mark out Orion's Belt. From there, fixed in the heavens, it was easy to find the stars that outline his sword hanging below, then to find the bright stars of Alderberan and Betelgeuse that shape his shoulders. You can navigate the sky map from there. No matter the hemisphere you are in, you can find Orion, unchanged since Ancient Greece. The stars that make him up are forever marked as his.

Unless you tell a different story. If you tell a different story, the eternal stars take on a completely different meaning. The Namaqua of South Africa tell a story that comically deflates the grandeur of the mighty hunter.

Alderberan was the husband of the Pleiades. One evening, he

took his spear and set out to hunt. In the distance, he spotted three fat zebras. He threw his spear, but missed. Just as he was about to fetch it, he spotted a hungry lion, patiently watching the same tasty zebras that he had been trying to hit. He froze. He dared not retrieve the spear (now lying on the far side of the zebras he had meant to hit) and risk the lion noticing him; and he dared not return home to his wives empty-handed, spear lost. So there he sits to this day, hungry and thirsty, in the cold night sky.

A different story transformed the stars of Orion's Belt into fat zebras, Orion's sword into a lost spear, Orion's shoulders into a lion and man, and pursued women into fierce wives. A story can change the stars.

◆

In his 2001 research discussed in the previous chapter, Dan McAdams found many different types of redemption narrative, many of which draw on powerful cultural narratives. He lists the four most powerful redemption narratives in North American culture: from rags to riches (upward mobility), from slavery to freedom (liberation), recovery (from an addiction or illness) and from sin to salvation (atonement). The last three are the most relevant to us here.

'Liberation' can include people being liberated from negative events in their lives or from aspects of their own personality. In 'recovery' redemption narratives, a person is torn from a good place, a place of virtue or innocence or privilege, either by their own actions or by other people and circumstances. They don't give up, though; they work to regain their place in society that they lost. Finally, 'atonement' narratives, McAdams says, have been a part of many famous people's transformative journeys and leadership personas. Here, the person has done wrong and seeks forgiveness. All are powerful and compelling and all emphasise the actions taken by the person to help themselves and improve their position.

We know that having a life story filled with a sense of agency and exploration, in which redemptive meaning is found in suffering, improves your mental health and wellbeing. Before we go on to how you can start changing *your* story, however, I need to give a caveat.

Our stories are not everything about us. As McAdams's theory reminds us, we are also a complex mix of genetics, dispositions and characteristic adaptations. If you are reading this in a state of deep distress and crisis, it's not the best time to try to reshape your inner narrative. There are, however, many professionals who can help. Seek them out first.

In a similar vein, as much as I am a passionate advocate of the transformative power of stories, I am a pragmatist. Life messes some people up badly. Genetics, circumstances, bad company, unlucky accidents – all can damage people very deeply. It would be naive to expect someone so battered by life to find a re-narration, on its own, helpful. That is not the individual's fault. A story cannot cure all that.

Noticing that stories have limits, though, is actually the point. Our memories are built around powerful emotions and the stories we build around both feel burnt into our souls. These stories become like the elephant in Chapter 8: we think we control them through the logical mind of our mahout. In truth, the stories can come to control us, without our even fully noticing that they're there. As we've seen with Kyle, Jacques, Sisanda, Sarel and Michael, their stories provided the secret selves that they hid away from the world and became the killer stories that ultimately led to their downfall. These stories can be so hidden that not even the killers themselves fully perceive them. 'Even today, I cannot say why,' muses Sisanda, when asked about the reason for some of his actions. 'If only I had realised ...' laments Jacques when talking about how his crimes evolved. They simply couldn't see their own stories. They knew something was wrong, but they didn't realise how bad, how big, their problem was. They couldn't see solutions that might be obvious to the outsider.

As I discovered, hunched over audio tapes and old notes, meaning is not something that is simply found. The killer stories were not directly transcribed from the interview tapes, whole and immediately obvious. Rather, stories are something you construct and create. You weave experiences and words and emotions into a chain of cause and effect which makes sense of the events. Meaning is not mined, it's moulded. Each murderer I spoke to claimed 'it's just the way I am', but that's not accurate at all. It would be truer to say 'this is how I've chosen to make meaning in my life'.

So how can you, the reader, avoid falling victim to your own version of a killer story? How can your secret selves become your ally rather than enemy?

American writer and historian Studs Terkel casts a long shadow over anyone who collects oral histories, makes podcasts or seeks to understand people through the stories they tell. In a career spanning the last half of the 20th century and into the 21st, he collected hundreds of stories from everyday people all over the United States. He shared these stories on his long-running radio show, in his many media appearances and in no fewer than 18 books. His Pulitzer Prize-winning book *The Good War* has spawned a series of mimics and changed the way we write about war. Even science-fiction and horror books have imitated his oral style.

Reflecting on his long career listening to stories, Terkel recalled that asking the average person to contemplate their life was unusual. He recounted a particular interview in the 1960s with a woman from the inner city living in low-income housing. After the interview, the woman asked him to replay her interview. He did, and she listened to her words echoed back to her in rapt attention. When the recording finished, she turned to Terkel and said, 'You know, I didn't know I thought that way.'

Terkel mused that 'recounting your story can be a revelation to yourself'. This was certainly my experience when I started serious storytelling. Nicole, too, noticed patterns in her story only when she spoke it aloud. Words that roar loudly in the confines of your skull suddenly quieten when written down or spoken. That's when you will really see, perhaps for the first time, what your thoughts are.

That's the first step: to get your story out of your head.

If you do want to pick someone to speak to, choose them carefully. Many of our closest friends and family have had a role in shaping our story and your story could affect your relationship with them. However, you don't need anyone else to get your story out. You can jot your story down on paper, start a private online document or even speak it aloud, alone in your room. Don't worry about structure and your writing skill. Do include emotions: put all your feelings in there. Just putting our feelings down on paper has been proven to have a positive effect on our levels of stress.

Writing your story down will create distance between you and the story that has been making its home in your head. This distance will empower you to change the story you tell yourself, setting you up for the next step.

Now that your story is outside your head, you have more power over it. It's time to start using that power. Put another way: you've acknowledged your secret self; now you need to start playing with them.

This second idea is best illuminated by the story of a little boy called James. He, and his parents, had come for help to an Australian called Michael White, one of the co-founders of narrative therapy. White's therapeutic practice involved work with everyone from prisoners to children, to couples and families. He rebelled against the idea that a client should simply follow blindly behind a therapist, a diagnosis or a technical interpretation. He believed everyone had the resources to deal with their challenges on their own terms, using their stories.

James had been diagnosed with Attention Deficit Hyperactivity Disorder (ADHD) and his parents were very worried. ADHD often manifests in childhood with symptoms of hyperactivity, impulsivity and lacking in attention. The symptoms can disrupt all the elements of a child's life: how they think, how they learn, their emotions and relationships. James – crashing things together, ignoring the adults, crawling under the therapist's desk and generally being a whirlwind of activity – was living up to his diagnosis: he was a 'tornado', White reports. The therapist described discussing James while bobbing up and down, as if riding a camel, as James played with his chair.

'He's taking his medication,' his parents lamented, 'but it's not enough. Surely there is more that can be done.'

'What sort of ADHD does he have?' asked White.

The parents looked at each other, nonplussed: 'We don't know.'

So White turned to James, who this far had ignored him utterly, and asked, 'What colour is your ADHD?'

James didn't know.

'Have you ever seen it? How do you know you've got it if you've never seen it?' the therapist asked.

At this point, White quipped, his parents must have been regretting coming to him for a second opinion, but James was interested, engaged. White continued by telling James about another one of his clients. 'I saw a boy called Freddy, and I think his ADHD might be the twin of your ADHD,' White said. He went into his filing cabinet and brought out a painting of a boy. 'Does this look like your ADHD?'

'Oh, yes, it looks familiar,' said James's parents, playing along.

All quickly came to a consensus that this ADHD was indeed a twin of James's ADHD.

What Freddy did to get the picture was very clever, White explained to James. He woke up one night without warning and caught his ADHD when it was off duty. Before his ADHD could jump back into his life, Freddy took a photo of ADHD in his mind. Then he went back to sleep and the next morning when he woke up he painted his ADHD.

'I wonder how you could get a picture of your ADHD?' the adults mused while James listened.

James thought for a bit, then said, 'I can wake myself up in the middle of the night and get a picture.'

His parents agreed that this was a really good idea, because once they'd got a picture of the ADHD, then everyone would know what to do about him.

Speaking to James's parents, White got them to practise asking James one simple question: 'Did you do it, James?' It wasn't an exercise they had to force James to do, but every morning when he woke up, they should ask him, 'Did you do it, James?' If James asked what they meant, his parents weren't to tell him; they just had to ask him the same question the next day: 'Did you do it, James?'

Off the family went.

On the first morning, James's parents asked him, 'Did you do it, James?'

James had no idea what they were talking about.

On the second day, they asked him, 'Did you do it, James?'

This time, James remembered, and said, no, he hadn't done it.

On the third morning, they asked him, 'Did you do it, James?'

And James said, 'Yes, I did it. I woke up in the middle of the night, and I saw my ADHD, and I took a picture of him in my mind.' James then sat down and drew his ADHD.

When he next went to see Michael White, James took along the picture of his ADHD. On seeing it, White said he could understand why James's life felt so out of control. It looked even fiercer than Freddy's. It was like some mutant ninja ADHD, White said. It was terrifying.

This picture, though, put up on the wall, helped them to start the conversation about what James's ADHD was up to. Now they could explore the impact that this ADHD was having: wrecking his relationships with teachers, ruining his friendships with his parents and having an impact on how James felt about himself. Most importantly, it would free James from blame, from the implication that he was a problem for himself and everyone around him. That James wasn't the problem, the ADHD was the problem.

'The person isn't the problem,' White stated, in what would become a key principle of narrative therapy, 'the problem is the problem.'

How freeing! Your problem isn't part of you. It's outside. Outside, you can work with it. Yet with this freedom comes responsibility: the responsibility for authoring your own story.

The fact that our truth is not set in stone, is ours to create, is both a burden and freedom. Luckily, you have all the tools of storytelling at your disposal. In his therapeutic practice, Michael White used the techniques of storytelling: mapping conversations (yes, a bit like the timeline of a crime), re-authoring storylines, revisiting old conversations and shaping new ones, allowing the person to define themselves differently and, ultimately, tell a different story about themselves. Even borrowing stories from our wider culture and applying them to your own life has been shown to improve people's wellbeing and resilience. Ideally, the community surrounding the person becomes part of this process, cementing and celebrating progress as the person's story is re-told.

When Nicole and I discussed this, she immediately mentioned that she saw this whenever she spoke to victims of crime. She reported losing count of the number of times she'd been told how powerful and healing it was for a victim or a family member of a victim to hear their story told in its entirety by someone else. She, like the narrative therapists, attributes this to a change in perspective.

When people hear their story told outside of their own heads, Nicole observed, they are forced to view it from another perspective and, suddenly, things that didn't make sense do and residual trauma that has lingered often starts to fade. If they are willing to dig deep enough, they might even acknowledge how the narratives they have been perpetuating in their own heads have extended the trauma they've experienced far beyond the point of necessity.

It doesn't feel like a revolutionary idea, does it? In fact, it feels so obvious, something you intuitively knew anyway: that your story can shape you, hurt you, or heal you.

How does this all relate to the killer stories? What would you do to overcome the engrained thoughts of a lifetime? What could you realistically do to change your secret self?

We know that stories are powerful, making sense of our lives and giving them direction. Existing in the twilight space between our conscious and unconscious lives, they are woven from our emotions and shape our beliefs.

Each killer story we discovered conjured a secret self into being. Each killer story served a purpose, helping the storyteller deal with tough lives and overwhelming emotions. The killer stories motivated them, drawing their power from the narratives in our culture.

As you read each story, you may even have had a glimmer of recognition. I would be surprised if anyone reading this, looking at their own stories honestly, would fail to detect the dark energy of a killer story glowing somewhere deep within.

So how do you stop being betrayed by your own killer story? How can we nurture our secret selves, turning them from saboteur to ally?

Here's how to kill a killer story, drawing on the insights from narrative psychology, and narrative therapy. For simplicity, these are summarised in numbered stages, although in reality the sequence is probably more complex and shifting. As McAdams says, life is messy and a story is neat.

1. See your story. Notice the story you're living, name the characters, trace its history. This creates distance between you and your story

2. Acknowledge that the story you were living is wrong. Until you do this, as often as you need to, you will stay trapped.

3. Reject the idea that enabled the story. This may be a belief about the world or yourself or other people, and will often be an idea you have taken on from significant others or society.

4. Acknowledge your agency. You are not a passive victim of fate. Accept that you can take action to change your situation and your story. Start by finding new, better, stories about yourself. Pick those that highlight positive aspects of your life.

5. Build your new story. You're the author. Build the characters and the plot. Commit your story to a purpose bigger than yourself. Best of all, commit it to something that benefits other people.

6. Practise your story. Agency is nothing if you don't use it. Talk about your story, write it, and when you're ready, act on it. Taking action helps embed your new story.

7. Draw others into your new story. Collect allies and inspirations – people you can tell your story to, someone who can support you, role models, even the

characters of films and books – to help inspire and support you on the journey.

8. Release the old story. There are many private and public ways to release yourself from a story that no longer serves you, one of which is forgiveness.

9. Grit. Through your story, then your actions, you are changing the adaptations of a lifetime. This won't be easy. Every time you think, I've done enough, I'll stop there – do more.

10. Keep telling a better story. Only a better story can kill a story. Your new story will probably never be a finished product. Rather, it is something you keep telling, and re-telling, to keep you strong as life changes about you.

Killer stories and what they tell us about our secret selves – isolation, revenge, disintegration, the other, outside, the fog and being the victim – are powerful. They tap into deep narratives in ourselves and our culture and can drive our actions.

Our stories aren't mirrors of our life, though. Rather, they shape the way we perceive it.

You've read how twisted perceptions can be baked into an inner story that spreads pain and darkness. Yet we also know that a redemptive story can make life more meaningful and happier. If we are able to change our stories, we open up new horizons in our lives.

The secret selves with which you populate your inner narratives can trap you or set you free. Whichever of these you choose to follow is up to you.

PART III
RESPONSIBILITY

11 Stefaans: Redemption

The crime

Although the Western Cape town of Worcester is the third largest in the province, it has managed to maintain a small-town feel. Its isolation may play a role in this: stand anywhere in Worcester, turn 360 degrees, and you'll see only majestic mountains all around, cradling the town in their rocky womb.

Residents of the town would be forgiven for thinking that those mountains could form a natural barrier of sorts, one that might protect them from the evils of the outside world. On 24 December 1996, though, senseless hatred and violence traversed those rocky barricades and arrived on their doorstep.

The 1996 festive season was filled with more hope for the historically dispossessed residents of Worcester than perhaps ever before. Although the country was still deep in the throes of massive change, the Truth and Reconciliation Committee process was underway. With it came building expectations for healing the wounds of the past. Perhaps if the secrets and violence that upheld apartheid in South Africa could be exposed, and the people who had carried out those acts brought into the light of day, then this new Rainbow Nation could be a reality?

Nelson Mandela, freed from prison after 25 years, was

president. His appointment clawed back some small semblance of the dignity ripped away from the vast majority of South Africans during apartheid.

Mandela had been a Struggle fighter but now, as the head of the nation, his message had evolved: the Struggle is over. Now is the time for us to join hands with all South Africans, regardless of race, and start to rebuild. In the minds of some white South Africans, however, the struggle was just beginning.

One of Mandela's inspiring speeches called on South Africans to embody the change they wanted to see in their country. For three men walking Worcester's streets on Christmas Eve that year, their backpack contents signified that the change they wished to see involved violence, death and destruction.

The Shoprite store in Kerk Street was open for business despite there having been an armed robbery there just three days before. The store was probably targeted because it was very busy in the build-up to Christmas and the tills were full. Similar criteria were used by the next group of criminals who targeted the store, with one significant difference – the robbers wouldn't have cared if the money had come from black or white people, but the men who targeted specific businesses in Worcester on the 24th were very well aware that the predominant demographic there was black and brown people.

On the 24th, cashiers and customers reported smelling a strong odour of ammonia. Many of the shoppers complained but the store was so busy in the festive-season buzz that no one took heed.

Ammonium nitrate was a commonly used component of explosive devices among terror groups in the 1990s and early 2000s. Many of the explosive devices used by the Irish Republican Army contained ammonium nitrate, for example, as did the Oklahoma City bomb, and the devices used in Bali in 2002 to kill 200 people in nightclubs there. Of course, those smelling the odour that day had no idea about this as their eyes watered from the smell. For most, ammonia was something used to clean the house, not to kill people.

The Felix family was getting ready to go on holiday that day.

Peter Felix was packing the family car in preparation, humming, picturing endless days of sunshine at the seaside. His eight-year-old daughter, Bianca, had accompanied her aunts to Shoprite to buy last-minute items for the trip.

When the phone rang inside the Felix house, at first Peter didn't answer it, not wanting to deal with whatever was on the other end that might break his peaceful mood. When it stopped and then almost immediately started ringing again, he sighed and trudged inside to pick it up.

At the other end of the line, his mother's voice sounded strange – tight, strangled, as though it may break at any moment. Dispensing with her usual greetings, his mother demanded to know her granddaughter's whereabouts. When Peter paused for longer than his mother could bear, she blurted out, 'There's been a bombing at Shoprite, Peter! Where is Bianca?'

Peter would later tell journalists that he couldn't remember how he had ended the call with his mother, or even how he'd made his way to Kerk Street, where a chaotic scene greeted him. Wails of pain and terror intermingled with shouts of various names – desperate calls from family members trying to find those from whom they'd been separated.

Police were already on the scene, and Peter pushed past the blockades they had put up. Nothing would stop him from finding Bianca. The Worcester SAPS was overrun that day, anyway, completely unprepared to deal with an incident of this magnitude in their town.

As zombie-like shoppers stumbled around in the street, their ears ringing, their vision blurred by blood and tears, Peter ran into the store. It was far from safe. No one knew how many devices had been planted, and another could go off at any time.

His most prominent memory of that day was how he couldn't seem to get his footing from the moment he stepped into the store. He slipped and fell many times as he rushed through the aisles looking for his daughter. Only later did he look down at his blood-soaked pants and realise what had made the floor so slippery.

In the throng of people, ambulances and horror, Peter was

unable to find Bianca. She was, in fact, already en route to hospital – badly injured, but alive, unlike four other people who had been in the store when the bomb, disguised in Christmas decorations, had exploded.

Two victims died in the store that day: 35-year-old Samuel Jalile and nine-year-old Andile Matshoba. Nine-year-old Juanita April died of a devastating stomach injury in hospital a few hours later, as did Xolani Matshoba, Andile's brother. Sweetness Busakwe, a fulltime cashier at the store, died some time later of injuries sustained in the bombing.

The three perpetrators were long gone. They would hide out in the bush for a few days, camping out of sight. Really, though, even if anyone had spotted them, it's unlikely they would have pinned them as the racist bombers: they looked like any other group of wholesome young men enjoying the outdoors. There were no skinheads or swastika tattoos as external indicators of the deep hatred that drove them.

As the three huddled down in the bush, waiting for the right time to head back to their home base, where their leader would give them instructions for their next mission, deep discontent grew among them. The youngest of the group would later admit that he had conflicting feelings about the results of their actions that day. He was disappointed that their kill rate had been so low, but when he heard that three children had been killed, he felt uneasy. It is perhaps this disquiet, or something else that lived, as yet, undiscovered in the young man's mind, that caused him to reach out to the investigating officer and hand himself over.

In January 1997, two of the group handed themselves over. A further two – the third who had been present on the day and one other person involved in the planning – were arrested shortly after.

It is difficult to calculate the true impact of the two bombs – the perpetrators had laid a second device, a few stores down from the Shoprite, near a pharmacy – that exploded in Worcester in December 1996. While we can count the number of dead – five – and the number of wounded – 67 – the number of lives changed is incalculable.

Peter Felix's medical-aid funds had run out long before his daughter was ready to be released from the hospital. He sold his house and two cars to pay for her treatment. His marriage did not survive the financial impact.

Lydia Busakwe never quite got over the death of her daughter, Sweetness.

Gertrude Louw, 72 years old at the time of the bombing, sustained head and ear injuries that required daily medication for the rest of her life. The worst pain, though, Gertrude said, was the memory of a woman covered from head to toe in blood after the bombs had gone off. No medication was available to stop that image appearing in her dreams, night after night.

The bombing of the Shoprite store in Worcester remains a deep scar on the mountain town. Even now, almost three decades later, for the primary, secondary and tertiary victims, the memory is as fresh as the day it occurred.

Much has happened since the day those three young men were handcuffed and led away, though – surprising, beautiful and deeply painful things that absolutely no one could have predicted.

Stefaans' killer story

Writing these killer stories, my secret fear was that a killer story could lie on someone like a curse, a self-inflicted, unshiftable blight on their personality and world. There wasn't much evidence to the contrary, and that felt pretty depressing. What hope was there for people to improve? There may be people who are irredeemably bad, but what about everyone else: muddling along, making mistakes, wanting to do better. Were we all locked into our narratives? Once we were living a story, could we ever live a different one?

This made Stefaans Coetzee's story an unexpected surprise, getting better and better at every turn. What surprised me more was that Stefaans was not a celebrity. In eternally optimistic and hope-hungry South Africa, more people should know his name. (Some recognised his previous moniker, the Worcester Bomber.)

Stefaans, a deeply religious man and a proud Afrikaner, has

come to realise that belief and culture can divide and he now seeks to transcend those divides. He has spoken a lot about his experiences so, before my brief conversation with him, I got to know him through podcasts, news items and YouTube.

Stefaans has the lean athleticism of a born distance athlete. In one interview he speaks about his childhood dream of running like his hero, Bruce Fordyce, the ultramarathon legend who won the 90-kilometre Comrades marathon nine times. Stefaans reminds me of him, with the same slight frame and intelligent face. I can't help but feel a kinship with him when he confesses this dream: I grew up in a marathon-mad family, spending childhood afternoons amusing myself at the finish lines of various cross-country and road races. As Stefaans' story unfolds, I find more common ground in our cultural heritage.

Let's take a step back, though, and tell the story from the beginning.

Just after Islamist bombs detonated in the London Underground in 2007, killing 52 people, as part of the English policing division that dealt with terrorism, I helped to clear out an old secure storage locker in the police force headquarters. In it, found photographs from a much earlier era – an Irish Republican Army bomb targeting a military band that had gone wrong and exploded while the two young Republicans were carrying it to the scene, just as they passed a town-centre bank.

Of course, I had seen violence committed by one human being on another: direct brutality, up close, with hands, ropes, knives, clubs, guns. Shocking as that is to see, the remains are still recognisably human. The bomb carriers' remains were something else, and filled me with a unique sense of horror. The human had simply vanished in the blast. I felt slightly nauseated by seeing the integrity of a human body so easily and utterly obliterated.

Planting a bomb has long been the weapon of the disempowered or aggrieved. South Africa has a long history of bomb planting, throughout its history and by all sides of the political spectrum. Growing up in 1980s and '90s in Johannesburg, we became familiar with the posters up in schools illustrating the appearance and shape of the weapons used by so-called terrorists: AK-47s, Makarov pistols, the various Soviet landmines and limpet mines for which we were to keep watchful eyes open. In high school, I was part of the school 'Dog and Bomb Squad', with a mission to check bins for bombs and keep dogs off the school grounds. I never found either, but I felt important doing this job protecting my peers.

As white South African boys, Stefaans Coetzee and I grew up in the same national context, with the same promise of conscription as soon as high school was done, being sent to fight the Border War in Namibia against the 'communist danger'. His home life, however, could not have been more different from my life of comfortable, stable security and caring parents.

Stefaans tells a striking anecdote from his early life. One day, when he was about five years old, his mother sent him out to buy sweets. Stefaans walked excitedly to the shop, thinking about what he was going to buy: fireballs for him and his older sister, so they could have a competition about how long they could keep the spicy treat in their mouths before spitting them out; and gobstoppers for his little sister.

When he arrived back home, his mother was gone. No one explained to young Stefaans where she had gone. 'You spend the rest of your life searching for something that wasn't there,' he muses, saying this event left a larger scar on him than his 18 years in prison. He still avoids sweets and the memories they evoke of that day.

That abandonment, that loss, had a profound effect on Stefaans. 'She just went,' he says, and in the struggle to understand, the young Stefaans wondered if it was his fault. Foremost, it left him with the question 'Why am I not loved?' This question marked a pivotal moment in his story. The feeling he wasn't loved and had been abandoned by his own mother haunted him. Stefaans says he used to hate birthdays, Mother's Day, Christmas, all because of that feeling.

As he got older, that question 'Why am I not loved?' started to loom larger and larger. 'You walk around with this question in you,' he says.

Stefaans' father was not abusive. He doesn't remember his

father ever hitting him, and fondly recalls himself and his sisters admiring his father's tattoos, turning him around and around so they could look at all the pictures. Rather, Stefaans' father sank deep into alcoholism.

He was about ten years old when he arrived home from school and found two women there waiting for him. His and his sisters' bags were already packed. From that point on, Stefaans lived in children's homes.

Stefaans reports few happy times in his childhood from then on. He tells an anecdote of being grabbed by a group of boys and thrown into a bath filled with hot water. As he leapt out, the tap caught his backside and gashed it, leaving a nasty scar.

The misery of living in a children's home, haunted by the question 'Why am I not loved?', was Stefaan's dominant narrative of this time in his life. Pausing, though, Stefaans reflects that this story blinded him to the goodness that was there – not just the fun of mischief with friends, but the deeper kindness shown by his carers. Stefaans recalls that the house mother's own son ate at the same table as all the other boys in the home. He wishes that he had appreciated at the time that she loved him as much as she did her own son.

Stefaans 'wasn't a sweet child', he reports. He says he was a bookworm and liked playing chess, but 'while there was that light in him, there was also that darkness'. He says that in the children's home you had to fight for everything you got. In this atmosphere of violence, Stefaans' frustration craved a violent outlet. However, when he got into fights at school he would get caned, so he and a group of the other boys used to go out on Friday and Saturday nights and beat up black people. This, he says, was acceptable in the culture of South Africa at the time. He said the police knew who they were, but no one got arrested. The only action he remembers being taken was later, when one of the men the boys attacked died. A peer Stefaans had gone out on these sprees with was arrested and, based on photographic evidence, imprisoned for murder.

The night-time mob assaults on innocent passersby were not enough to satisfy the anger in Stefaans: 'I needed to hurt more.' This was, he says, 'what the bomb makers dialled into. Ultimately,

I had to commit murder because I wanted to hurt more people.'

Although Stefaans was not a serial murderer, you can see the patterns his story shares with those of Jacques, Sisanda, Kyle and Michael, and even the rapist Sarel: another abandoned child, in an unkind world; another person with a deep sense of not being worthy, filled with growing anger and resentment. Stefaans tells a story filled with inner characters who, if you wished to name them, would not sound out of place in any of the other killer stories: the Absent Mother, the Helpless Father, the Violent Peers. It was the same killer story of loneliness, revenge and (waiting in the wings) the other, outside, all ultimately adding up to the sense that he was living a 'condemnation script' as a victim of his circumstances.

Stefaans, like all human beings, was also drawing on the cultural narratives surrounding him to build his own story. In his case, it was the apartheid culture that accepted violence against black people and glorified military struggle.

The other, outside entered his life in the form of Israel Vision. His introduction to the white supremacist group came via a friend whose father was a South African rugby legend. Stefaans comments wryly that 'growing up in South Africa at the time, the first thing people would ask about you is, "What position do you play in a rugby team?" So the character was very attractive, and he was a cell leader.'

Every weekend this man would give lessons and train the boys in the philosophy of the Israelites, which was deeply racist and scaffolded with religious verse. The religion they preached was drawn from their reading of the Old Testament. They rejected the teachings of Jesus and the New Testament, even Christmas.

With hindsight, Stefaans realises that they quoted biblical verses out of context to justify their own views and visions. He recalls a particular set of verses being used to justify the murder of a black person by a white person. To a young boy whose experience of apartheid South Africa was one where the police didn't care about him and his friends attacking black people for entertainment, this made sense. It chimed with his own experience and drew him deeper into his hatred.

In this atmosphere, the violence and racism of his early life became distilled in the character of the White Wolf, a character that gave him purpose and acceptance.

Stefaans moved in with the white supremacist group on their farm and Israel Vision's teachings became less important to him than the community they gave him: 'It was less about the philosophy than it was about the search for love.'

In the run-up to South Africa's first democratic elections in 1994, a growing wave of resistance surged in white supremacist groups. Stefaans comments that the groups wanted more than white independence and dominance; they were 'super-racist'. They wished not only to derail the progress towards a new South Africa, they wanted to kill. Stefaans become a member of the Israel Vision sabotage groups, tasked with this mission of violent resistance.

They started with blowing up electricity pylons and the like. However, Stefaans comments, small acts of sabotage in the rural hinterland of South Africa only got a few lines in a small article in the local newspaper. 'To get your voice as a terrorist,' he says, 'you have to kill people.' The leaders of the group set a date by which 'heads must roll'. This pleased Stefaans.

The Gunston 500 was a popular surfing contest in the 1990s. Stefaans and a co-conspirator, Cliffie, took inspiration from the name and agreed to kill 500 people apiece. This gave him the opportunity to start his work. As Stefaans explains, he was living the words of the old South African national anthem: 'At thy call we shall not falter, / Firm and steadfast we shall stand. / At thy will to live or perish, / O, South Africa, dear land.' In his mind, he had become the soldier willing to kill and die for the defence of his country and his people.

The leaders set the date for the attack as 24 December 1996: Christmas that year would be covered with a pall of shock, death and trauma.

In the run-up to the attack, Stefaans noticed that their leader, Jan, was nervous.

I remember that day, he was very scared. When he walked

past me, I could see he was scared. I think he didn't want to
do it but didn't have the will to say, 'I can't.' [Ruefully] I was
too dumb to say I didn't want to do it either.

On Christmas Eve 1996, Stefaans, Jan and two other members of
their cell went to plant their bombs. Stefaans placed his outside
the Narotam Pharmacy in Worcester, which had plenty of glass to
suddenly become razored bullets as the bomb detonated.

He and the others fled into the bush, to a hidden training camp
which had a feeling of adventure to the young Stefaans: 'Now you
are part of the war. You are Tarzan and Rambo.'

Stefaans was initially disappointed by the result of the bomb
blasts. They killed only four people initially (a fifth victim died later)
and injured a further 67. However, while in hiding, he heard that his
bomb had killed children. This was not the war he had wanted to
wage. His inner narrative couldn't justify this. 'The youngest victim
was nine … That is just a child. That's really young.' So, unknown to
his fellow fugitives, Stefaans contacted the investigating officer and
handed himself over.

I never told them. [I] feared my death … Later I was proud
that I made the right choice, then I didn't care any more.

He later discovered that another of the bombers had also surren-
dered to the police, and the other two were captured soon after.
Their leader, Jan, was captured after fleeing to Namibia.

Stefaans' surrender and confession did not, however, change his
inner narrative. He was still the White Wolf and, arriving in prison,
his views were so racist and extreme the other inmates dubbed him
'Hitler'. Stefaans still saw himself as a hero of his volk, absolutely
sure of his rightness, and joined with the other whites who shared
his racist views to create an informal gang.

In prison, he started to write to other white supremacists all
over the world. 'In prison, one thing you have is time … I began
to believe in those groups,' he says, and rattles off names familiar
to me from my time in counter-terrorism: Kombat 18, the KKK,
White Pride Worldwide. 'Everything white, white, white, white.'
His philosophy started to change from 'boer rights' to 'white rights'.

Stefaans designed tattoos for others in this global white supremacist network.

> I wouldn't even let a black warden clean my cell, I was
> so full of hate ... I didn't even care how my words might
> hurt another person, even in the new regime [South Africa
> post-1994].

This is the point at which, more or less, every previous killer story
in this book came to me: with the murderer in prison, at the nadir,
the lowest point, of his narrative.

True-crime tales end even sooner, usually. We find that so
satisfying: the bad guy is caught and locked up. It evokes our old
cultural narratives of how we deal with wrongdoing and evil: lock
the monster in the dungeon and leave it there forever. The end.

It isn't the end, though, not in real life. The person goes on living
and, like every living thing, changes.

'Long is the way and hard, that out of Hell leads up to light,'
wrote John Milton in 1667 in his epic poem *Paradise Lost*. Stefaans'
story shows us how hard such a journey can be.

It starts, like any journey, with a first step or, for Stefaans, with
small meetings and kindnesses.

In South African prisons, the prison gangs have different roles:
the 27s help support and enforce the codes of the other gangs, the
26s and the 28s. Dubbed 'the men of blood', the 27s are the most
violent of the prison gangs. The boss of the 27s in Stefaans' prison,
Papa Red, invited the newly imprisoned youngster into his cell and
explained the rules to him. According to Stefaans, he explained
'how [I] should survive in prison. I wouldn't have got through
without this person.'

It baffled him as to why this black gang boss should care about
the fate of a young white racist.

This event was joined by others.

In the years from 2003 to 2007, Stefaans recalls being moved
around between prisons and court appearances, and being locked
in a cell without food. A group of black prisoners gave him food,
unasked: little round sandwiches with jam in them.

Later still, he decided to return to his studies. A communal cell is noisy and, usually, prisoners would go to the toilets to study in peace. Stefaans' black cellmates turned their radios down so that he could study comfortably. Stefaans says he hated the black prisoners' taste in music and did not like the people but then they treated him with consideration and kindness. Why are they doing that? he wondered. They should hate me. I want them to hate me. It gives me energy. Now I have no excuse to hate them.

Why, indeed, would black prisoners help a racist? Not once, but over and over again. We can only guess. Maybe they were trying to avoid conflict. Maybe other people saw glimmers of hope in Stefaans' character and wanted to help him. Maybe it was simple, stubborn, human kindness. What is interesting from a narrative perspective is that Stefaans started to notice. His previous narrative, which proclaimed that black people were less worthy, and that he was a victim of the world, would have encouraged him to ignore these incidents. As they accumulated, though, they started to chip away at his old narrative. He started to look back at his life and see things he previously hadn't noticed, like the orphanage mother who fed him the same food as her own son.

Then there were the prison staff who, as Stefaans puts it, 'trapped him' with books. Stefaans has always been a voracious reader and a prison section head decided to exploit this interest to help Stefaans' rehabilitation. He told Stefaans that if he cleaned a certain section, he could get books.

'I was a big reader,' said Stefaans, 'but was really interested in thrillers or similar.' The section head widened Stefaans' literary diet – specifically, the famous management tome *Who Moved My Cheese?* Stefaans identified with the main character, a mouse whose cheese had been taken, a metaphor for finding new goals in a changing world. 'Apartheid was my cheese,' he reflects, and with that having changed, he needed to change too.

The warders fed him more self-help books – *The Seven Habits of Highly Effective People*, for example – and then started to set him questions, quiz him, invest in his learning. Stefaans reflects, with amazement, that prisoners and warders 'bonded together' to help him. 'I couldn't believe so many people wanted to help me.'

And so his narrative started to change.

Notwithstanding this, 'I was still a racist,' says Stefaans. Then, five years into his prison sentence, he met Eugene de Kock. Labelled 'Prime Evil', and a symbol of the crimes of apartheid, De Kock had been the commanding officer of the apartheid government's network of police death squads, funded by the government, and tasked to kill the so-called terrorists of Nelson Mandela's African National Congress (ANC). He had been convicted of six murders and 89 other crimes; and he disclosed hundreds more in his testimony to the Truth and Reconciliation Commission. He had been sentenced to 212 years plus two life terms.

Stefaans was in awe of De Kock. He couldn't quite believe he was sitting so close to his idol who, like him, had killed black people. He anticipated the white-supremacist icon of media portrayal, 'but when I spoke with him, he gave me the opposite.'

De Kock read only the Bible, the Psalms, and

> he spoke about forgiveness a lot – so much that it started
> to irritate me. For me, it didn't work. I didn't think I was
> a racist. I was a proud Boer hero, fighting for my people,
> answering The Call.

Then De Kock challenged Stefaans. Just as Stefaans had built his narrative using the cultural stories that were swirling around him, De Kock broke his narrative using one of the same cultural stories.

For Afrikaners, the second Boer War is the cauldron in which their folk identity was born. They resisted the might of the British Empire at its peak in their second Freedom War and paid a terrible price. Struggling to contain the Afrikaners' guerrilla warfare, the British Empire sent captured Boer men overseas into exile, about 25 000 of them. Women and children, however, were housed in 45 concentration camps and more than 26 000 women and children perished in these tented camps from malnutrition, disease and negligence. The moral stain on the British Empire was deep, and changed both Imperial and South African history.

The memory of the concentration camps was a fire that helped forge the Afrikaner people. It was almost holy. De Kock turned this on Stefaans. 'The woman and children of the Second Freedom War will accuse you,' De Kock said. 'You're no better than their killers, or the ANC killers that you claim to fight.'

Stefaans' narrative of his righteous killing was deeply undermined. 'I became what I hated,' he says, and this made him angry. But this anger fuelled the next change.

It was Eugene de Kok who helped Stefaans write his first letter to the Supreme Court, saying that he wanted to ask for forgiveness from his victims.

Here we come to the part of the story that some readers will find difficult. We are soaked in narratives of evil people manipulating the system for their own ends. True crime often relishes the idea of bad people being mercilessly punished for eternity, and social media simmers with suspicious anger every time parole for a murderer is mentioned. We simply don't hear the stories of murderers following the hard path that, out of hell, leads to heaven.

The path that Stefaans followed was more gruelling than any I have heard. Each time I thought he was going to stop in his efforts towards forgiveness and reconciliation and say, 'I've done enough,' he pushed on. 'Forgiveness isn't a word, it's an action,' he says.

Through his actions, Stefaans now chose gradually to erase the character of the White Wolf. In its place, a new character was being created: the Repentant. The Repentent knew he had done wrong and was willing to reject his past, apologise and repent of his old ideas, and make things better.

Stefaans saw the effect his story had on other people: the people he had killed, injured and traumatised, and the people he continued to mistreat due to his racism. He saw it was wrong and needed to change.

The process of changing it started 2007. Supported by prison staff, he began by taking a year-long course in restorative justice. Restorative justice encourages people who have committed crimes to take responsibility for their actions and understand the harm they have caused, to give them an opportunity to redeem themselves and to discourage them from causing further harm. Their victims are active parts of this process, facing the person who hurt them, helping to hold them to account.

Over the years this qualification was joined by others: in anger management, life skills, HIV/AIDS, drug awareness, and so on. In the meantime, Stefaans kept pursuing his mission to apologise to his victims – not just apologise though, and he returns to this point again and again:

> It is not enough to say sorry. You have to say *why* you are sorry. You have to reject the beliefs that made you do wrong.

Almost as soon as his inner journey began, though, Stefaans hit the lowest point in this story. His nadir was the news announcing his possible release as part of a presidential pardon, and then learning shortly afterwards that he was not to be granted this pardon. He had secretly hoped to be released one day, and the announcement 'gave me false hope'. Being offered a release from prison, pain and punishment, only for it to evaporate so quickly afterwards, must have hurt.

This marked another change in Stefaans: he accepted he would die in prison. 'It was only when I made peace that I would die in prison that things became easy,' he says.

The acceptance of this fate, this condemnation, did not lead Stefaans into apathy. Quite the opposite.

The people of the town Stefaans had bombed, on the other side of the country from where he was sitting in Pretoria Central Prison, had created victim support groups. Hundreds had been caught in the waves and ripples of the tragedy, and this group had banded together. They now sent two representatives to go and speak to this young man who was wanting, apparently, to say sorry.

Stefaans' account suggests the representatives were not naive idealists. They took the business of forgiveness seriously and they were not going to be fobbed off with glib apologies. They returned to the people of Worcester and encouraged their fellow townsfolk to 'hear him out', because Stefaans wanted to say sorry to everyone: not just to a representative, but to everyone he had directly hurt, to the whole town.

Stefaans says that initially the prison service didn't take his desire to meet everyone seriously. Moreover, they had no idea how they would do this. Stefaans was a maximum-security prisoner who didn't just want to write a letter. No one had ever wanted to apologise to their victims on this scale before: 'Bombing is a public act, so my apology had to be public.'

The prison service wrote to the townspeople of Worcester saying that if they could get the funding to come to Pretoria Central Prison, then they would arrange the visit. There were many victims, and perhaps they were not expecting that a small rural town would be able to arrange for many hundreds of people to travel all that way. In two days, however, the churches of Worcester had raised enough money to hire an entire train.

In 2009, this 'Peace Train' set out to Pretoria to meet Stefaans.

The logistics were extensive and thoughtful. Psychologists on the train prepared the people to meet someone they had never seen but who had changed their lives forever. They divided the passengers into groups: those who wanted to forgive, those who did not forgive, and those who were not sure. Stefaans would meet with them all, separately. To each he would give the same apology.

'I was never so scared as on that day,' Stefaans says. Facing not just one person you hurt but a whole hall filled with people who have every reason to hate you is terrifying.

He made notes of what he had to say and kept to the list, so nothing was missed. When he faltered, he says, a prison psychologist standing near him would place a hand on his back, reassuring him and helping him continue.

While he was apologising, Stefaans was not expecting forgiveness:

> Forgiveness is not my choice. It is their choice. I need to say sorry, but it's up to them whether they forgive.

He had apologised to the people who travelled on the Peace Train, those he had left injured or bereaved. Stefaans wanted to do more, though. He explained that his bomb hadn't just touched those he had hurt or their families and the families of those he had killed. It

191

had changed a town: the women who worked in the shopping centre, the nurses who had dealt with the wounded, the emergency service workers who removed the dead from the scene. 'I traumatised all of them,' Stefaans says, linking this to the psychological trauma of apartheid:

> You didn't have to be directly affected physically to have had emotional and psychological scars or emotional and psychological wounds.

Stefaans wrote an open letter to the town. It was read out there, on Reconciliation Day, 16 December, in 2011. One of his victims released a white dove, a symbol of peace.

That year was the high point for Stefaans. 'I decided to live my dreams in prison,' he says, and he started writing stories and poems. He passed his matric. He ran 67 kilometres on a treadmill for Madiba Day, one kilometre for every one of his victims.

In lockstep with his transformation inside himself and inside prison walls, Stefaans was still wanting to keep finding ways to apologise to the town he had bombed. So, two years later, wearing the bright orange of a maximum-security prisoner, Stefaans got permission to go to Worcester.

Surrounded by prison officials, he walked through the shopping centre he had bombed. He spoke to a hall of a thousand people to say sorry for what he'd done to their town. He heard some say, 'Stefaans, I hate you for what you have done.' Looking at the film of that day, the emotional toll is clear in the eyes and faces of everyone there. You see weeping victims and Stefaans looking dull with shock, drained.

Then Stefaans went back to his cell. He did not want parole. He did not want anyone to think that he was saying sorry just to get out of prison.

The experience had an enormous impact.

> It took me two or three months to recover emotionally from the experience, but I was free. Not free from prison, like, free within myself.

For while he had been performing these external deeds of forgiveness and reconciliation, he'd also been doing work inside himself. He had been, through forgiveness and with support, rewriting his internal narrative.

This took eight long years of work supported by a combination of social workers and psychologists. 'When I showed I wanted to change, they really backed me,' he says.

I express some surprise at his willingness to seek help: people instinctively avoid challenging their own deeply held thoughts and beliefs, much less exposing their own failures to others.

> BH: Why did you do that?
> SC: I'm very selfish. If I am offered help, I will take it.
>   [Laughing]

It is this willingness to open himself to others, to reject the killer story of loneliness, that seems to set Stefaans apart. The Repentant didn't simply leap into being. Yes, it borrowed the best from people it met. Yes, it was kept alive by Stefaans' unrelenting commitment. But it was also nurtured into being by a host of others.

Stefaans' work on his narrative could be seen to have three aspects. First, he had to let go of the inner characters of other people who had hurt him. He did this, he says, through forgiveness. Describing an early restorative justice session where he and the other participants were asked to make a list of people they hated, the others came with a name or two, he says, but 'I had a long, long list'. He had to forgive each of these people for any hurt they had done and so let go of the internal characters: the Absent Mother, the Helpless Father, the Violent Peers. This eased their influence over his narrative.

Next, he had to 'forgive God for the circumstances I was placed in and the effect that this had on my life'. What a powerful way to reject the condemnation scripts that sink so many other narratives, that sense that you are a helpless victim in an unfriendly world! Through forgiving the universe that had put him in prison, Stefaans took his control back.

Finally, Stefaans had to forgive himself. His apologies, meeting his victims both in a group and as individuals, were a public rejection of the character of the White Wolf. As part of this work, Stefaans forged strong relationships with a handful of his victims. The people he had hurt became his supporters.

He tells the story of Olga who, caught by his bomb, suffered life-changing injuries. She struggled to walk, which left her unable to care for her children, whom she sent to live with relatives. She didn't want to forgive Stefaans yet eventually she did, despite the pain she was still suffering. She said to other members of the victim support group that they should at least listen to Stefaans, hear him out. It was she who released the white dove on the day in 2011 when Stefaans' apology was read out; and she was there when he visited the town two years later. Stefaans came to call her 'Mama Olga'. Now she messages Stefaans when her injuries hurt her, teasing him, and they draw strength from each other. 'She is big for me,' says Stefaans.

The Repentant had forgiven and had been forgiven, and to keep that character nourished, Stefaans continued to be an advocate of restorative justice. He developed the course for those serving life sentences that they had to pass before being released on parole: 'A lot make mistakes, [but] some make a choice to be better.'

It would be tempting to imagine that Stefaans made the process easy for prisoners who had taken that choice to be better. This imagining would be wrong. Unflinching in his commitment to genuine restorative justice, he describes the surprise from another prison when he sent a rapist back from one of his courses early, failing him. Asked why, he said, 'He said he was sorry, but he didn't understand what he was saying sorry for.' It has to be more than empty words for Stefaans; it's about lasting actions. '[When I see someone] changing over time, then I know it's real.'

In doing this, Stefaans seems to have transcended the inner character of the repentant sinner, to become harnessed to a higher sense of purpose: that of forgiveness and redemption. This replaced the purpose and belonging the White Wolf initially gave, all those years ago. Harnessed to this new purpose, he seemed determined to share the message and pass on his learning. In the language of narrative psychology, he committed himself to a new, generative character: someone who produces something for the future. Given his reconciliation with the God he once rejected and his deep religious belief, something like 'The Disciple' would seem an appropriate name for this new character. He is committed to the philosophy of forgiveness and redemption, using it to tackle every fresh challenge.

The next challenge came unexpectedly.

Stefaans had never expected freedom and hadn't wanted parole lest people thought he was trading an apology for freedom. Yet his turn came to be considered for parole. He got no special treatment and followed the standard parole process.

While he wanted freedom, he knew that being free would bring new challenges. He had seen many of his fellow prisoners released after having served long sentences but 'ninety-four of a hundred go back', he estimates. Why did this happen? He had quizzed fellow so-called 'lifers' who, after tasting freedom, found themselves rapidly back in prison. 'I went out with a lot of anger,' reported one.

So Stefaans was again working with a psychologist because 'I decided to go out with all my issues resolved, with my mother, with the members [Correctional Services staff], with the gangs'. He wanted to ensure that the anger a long imprisonment could cause did not replace the anger of his youth.

When his parole hearing came, his victims were among those advocating his release. And after 18 years, six months, five weeks and one day Stefaans was let out of prison. On his first day of parole, he asked to hear a child laugh, so he went with a prison officer and parked outside a nursery school, just to hear the joyous noises bubbling over the wall. Then he had his first ice cream in a long time. For the first time in almost 19 years, he walked on grass, saw a flower, a tree, a woman; everything was beautiful. He says, laughing, that for years after his release, 'I never saw an ugly woman.'

Life outside was not, however, a simple joyful reunion. Everything had to be learnt: how a cellphone works, how to use a debit card for purchases, how to keep your past behind you. Stefaans relentlessly, seriously and systematically focused on the challenge of being alive with a history like his, once again following his plan for helping his story grow.

He started by finding more characters to learn from. Having seen most released lifers return to prison, Stefaans wanted to find others who had made the choice to do better – and he succeeded. He reels off a list of names of men who left long sentences and succeeded in rebuilding their lives, even becoming successful. These success stories became Stefaans' role models, forming part of the network of people Stefaans drew help from. With their input and support, he could keep rewriting his story.

Fuelling his progress, as was the case years before in prison, was his stubborn commitment to his higher purpose. He noticed with surprise that the country's 'complexes had grown, almost like we hated each other more'. His personal journey of forgiveness and reconciliation was one that the whole country needed to undertake.

> Forgiveness and reconciliation are not the same thing. I can forgive you, then I go on my path, and you go on yours. Reconciliation is you and me saying, 'Let's build together.' South Africa forgave but did not move on. While forgiveness is in the heart, reconciliation is building the relationship.

Stefaans continues to live his new redemption narrative in the new South Africa. Through books, podcasts and radio broadcasts, he continually advocates forgiveness. His advocating that white people apologise for the ills of apartheid has earned him hate mail, writers outraged at any suggestion of an apology for apartheid complicity. He has received death threats. Stefaans knows his path means people may kill him but

> I can't let other people drive me. I'm not scared about getting killed. I can't let other people live my life for me.

Stefaans' rhetoric of forgiveness remains backed by action. Apart from helping establish a Christian radio station, he started a community farming project, creating 50 vegetable tunnels. He's gone on to build a classroom, create a dam, and donate three 10 000-litre rainwater tanks, all invaluable in the semi-arid South African landscape.

He helps host regular shared dinners between black and white churchgoers. He forgave his mother, the source of that painful wound all those years ago. He finally fulfilled his childhood athletic dream and ran the Comrades Marathon. He insists, though, this was not something he did for his own glory: he ran it for Jesus, and he ran it for Olga. When injury struck him on that hilly course between Pietermaritzburg and Durban, his victims leapt into his mind: 'If I give up, then I disappoint 67 people – my victims. I can endure the pain I gave them for a short while.' His run raised money for them, and Olga received his medal.

On race day, Stefaans was struck by the sense of community stretched all along the 90-kilometre route: 'You see complete peace in South Africa,' he says, all the races mingling happily; 'why can't we be like that every day?'

In a world that can seem so complicated, all problems too deeply rooted to do anything about, Stefaan's most simple call to action is that we talk to each other.

> Just sit down and talk and respect what the other person has gone through, and the story they have to tell. Because the pain isn't talked about, we live in an angry world. We need stories of hope.

He says he would love to see his victims' stories written in all the languages of the Rainbow Nation so their experience is seen and respected.

Stefaans describes his redemption as being due to 'indescribable grace'. I asked him what this meant to him.

> I had opportunities that not everyone could have: Papa Red's protection until I could find my feet; unbelievably good social workers and psychologists; an amazing section head; the victims' open hearts. It feels like God commissioned the universe to help me change. Every open door led to the next one. In prison, there is no better place to find yourself.

Stefaans' story turns the circumstances that would make another person curse their fate into a blessing.

Stefaans, unsurprisingly for a lifelong lover of books, remains a prolific writer. Apart from regular book reviews, he has released short stories on pretty much every Afrikaans literature platform. Writing anonymously, he's been shortlisted for short-story prizes. Then there are his books: four, going on five.

I wonder what part Stefaan's writing played in his process of self-forgiveness. Did writing his story help with this?

Writing has been part of his redemption, he says, and part of his leaving his former self behind. Writing is another way Stefaans is pulling his narrative into the future.

> Last year I went on a mission to make peace with myself, my past. My new book focuses on this. I'm not my past. I needed to make peace with it, otherwise I will become a victim of my past. Whenever a bomb explodes somewhere, it reminds me how I was. Writing is the medium [in which] I can be me, without being a bomber.
>
> I decided to love my past. The community work is the outcome of that love. Telling my story helps others to believe in white and black peace. It gives people hope. It gives meaning to the hardships the victims went through.

He has spoken a lot about his journey. He's written the books he wanted to write about his old life. At the end of 2025, he says, he will stop telling the story of his past and focus on his future. He has a family now, and he wants to spend more time with them, appreciating the second chance at life he has been given.

Listening to him, my feeling is that his story will keep unfolding, growing, evolving, into the future.

How did Stefaans create his redemption narrative?

We human beings are not always aware of why we act as we do. In addition to this, we are, to an extent, hardwired to believe that we are right. There's plenty of psychological literature and research about the cognitive biases we employ to persuade ourselves that whatever our decisions were, they were the right decisions to make.

Research emphasises time and again how hard it is for people to change. We protect our deeply held beliefs as if an attack on our most valued ideas is the same as an attack on ourselves. The stories we tell ourselves about ourselves have built up over time. We repeat our stories to ourselves, consciously and unconsciously. So the process of breaking down our stories about ourselves, the narratives that create our identity, is a hard one.

Even when we know those narratives are faultlines in our lives, threatening to break the ground open under our feet, we cling to them. Kyle, for example, avoided creating a narrative at all. He let his inner story rest in obscurity and accepted a superficial version that didn't come to terms with the brutal facts of what he had done. The killer stories the men in this book lived all represent condemnation scripts, the downward slide into tragedy. Many of them understood what their stories were doing to them, yet they struggled to break free. Many expressed a wish for some kind of redemption. Michael said he 'protected children' by his decision to 'work with the police' and longed for reconciliation with his biological family. Sisanda wore an AIDS awareness badge and was still nurturing his dream of being a pastor. Jacques said his participation in interviews with researchers was all part of his journey to find out more about himself and why he committed his crimes. Sarel spoke about writing a book on the occult to help young people like himself who were trapped in the occult.

We find it hard to approach these statements with an open mind. We want to dismiss them as things said to make these men look better in others' eyes. We are made uncomfortable by the fact that a person who took so many other people's dreamt-of tomorrows should want to think about his own tomorrows. We mistrust anyone's ability to climb out of such a deep pit, to become a better version of themselves, sincerely and truly.

At the same time the serial murderers were sharing their stories with me, Stefaans was starting the hard work of turning his condemnation into redemption.

How did he do this? While there's no doubt that luck played

some part in Stefaans' journey, it would be too simplistic to put his redemption down to this. When you combine his story with insights from narrative psychology, some clear patterns emerge.

1. See your story. Stefaans started by noticing the story he was living. He saw the bones of his story through the fog. He traced how it grew through the abandonment of his childhood, the inner character of the White Wolf becoming a channel for his anger and hurt. This realisation helped to create distance between himself and the story.

2. Acknowledge the story you were living is wrong. His debates with Eugene de Kock, the kindness of other prisoners, the support of warders and the awareness of the pain he had caused all led to Stefaans' realising that his racism, his identity as White Wolf, was wrong. This started him on the journey of changing them both.

3. Reject the idea that enabled this story. For Stefaans, it was apartheid and the ingrained cultural narratives that were woven into his story.

4. Acknowledge your agency and find better stories. Woven like a thread through his redemption narrative is Stefaans' commitment to action. Not content simply to think about forgiveness, for example, he sought it out. He acted to get help from those around him. He read and gathered knowledge. He embraced his agency, throwing himself into the work of building a better story. He did not passively accept the narrative of his life. He focused on aspects of himself and his life that contradicted the old story and set a more positive tone: his love of books, his idealism, his dream to run the Comrades Marathon, his lack of fear of standing alone and forging his own path. These became the seeds of the new story.

5. Build your new story. Stefaans the book lover became

the author of this story. He looked back on his life and found all the characters that had helped him. He committed himself to a redemptive plot. He tied his story to something greater than himself: the search for forgiveness and reconciliation in the new South Africa. This was not the self-serving commitment of a terrorist or a serial murderer who seeks to boost their status through their commitment to an idea. This was a purpose that was explicitly about others, the church and community around him, and what might benefit them.

6. Practise your story. In Stefaans' re-narration of his life he talked to therapists, wrote many letters of apology, created poetry, spoke to the people he had hurt (over and over again), ran marathons for charity, gave lectures on reconciliation ... His actions helped him become this new story.

7. Draw others into your story. Stefaans collected allies and inspirations throughout his journey. These people gave him support when he flagged, guidance when he felt lost and role models on which he could build a better inner character for himself. Even the wider cultural narratives of the new South Africa were drawn into rebuilding his story. Other people also gave Stefaans a safe space in which to speak about his experience, and so help to reshape it. Through the process of reconciliation, some of Stefaans' victims become his advocates and supporters. And when he found himself on parole, he realised he needed a new set of inspirations and allies, 'lifers' who had made a new life outside, new voices for forgiveness in the church and society. He actively drew on them to scaffold and mould his story.

8. Release the old story. Stefaans achieved this in a particularly powerful way: through forgiveness. He

forgave himself, those who had wronged him, and God. He asked for forgiveness for the wrongs he had done to others. The rituals he performed to get this forgiveness were suited to the needs of each element of the story. He forgave himself and God in private, and he sought forgiveness in public from those he had so publicly injured.

9.   Grit. Stefaans showed grit again and again: when he started his journey to forgiveness, when he sought forgiveness, when he reconciled himself to life in prison, when he left prison, and as he continues to face opposition and challenges in life. He kept trying and he kept going.

10. Tell a better story. Stefaans' journey didn't end with the youthful White Wolf. He changed the plot from contamination and condemnation to redemption and agency. His story moves on, it grows, and listening to it gives us hope that the world can be a better place.

Acknowledgements

Dr Brin Hodgskiss – thank you for responding to that random tweet from that random podcaster way back when. Your passion for stories has made me see my own story differently. You've made this book writing process fun and far less stressful than I believed possible. I'm incredibly proud to be sharing a cover with you. As a wise man once said: onward and upward!

Gill Moodie/Guardian of the Stories – thank you for taking the chance on our strange little idea about murderers. Working with you has been an absolute pleasure and your input has elevated this book superbly. I cannot wait to tell more stories with you.

Nicole Engelbrecht

◆

I'd like to thank the people without whom I would never have had the conversations in this book: Micki Pistorius, Mark Welman, Gérard Labuschagne, Elmarie Myburgh, Dave Beyers and all the members of the South African Police Service and the South African Correctional Services I met on the way.

Secondly, thank you, Nicole Engelbrecht. I couldn't have wished for a better, and more ethical, collaborator. The journey was great fun! Gill Moodie, Tracey Hawthorne and the whole team at

Jonathan Ball Publishers also have my gratitude for making these stories even better (and not letting me hide from myself).

Thank you to the friends and colleagues from my university days until now who were part of the experience, helped shape my thinking and were the brave souls who tolerated my talking to them endlessly about my ideas.

The final thank you will always be to my family in South Africa, and to Claire and Adam here in Cambridge, for letting me know that I make you proud.

Brin Hodgskiss

Sources

Athens, L (1997) *Violent Criminal Acts and Actors Revisited.* University of Illinois Press

Bosch, B (2018) 'Episode 37: Stefaans Coetzee (die Witwolf bomplanter en versoeningskonsultant)' on *Narratief met Bouwer Bosch,* Apple Podcasts, https://podcasts. apple.com/gb/podcast/narratief-met-bouwer-bosch/ id1278922382?i=1000419313677

Campbell, J (2003) *The Hero's Journey: Joseph Campbell on his life and work* (3rd ed). HarperCollins

Coetzee, S (2023) *Onbeskryflike Genade.* Lux Verbi Books

Coetzee, S and Steenkamp, A (2019) *Wit Wolf: Die Worcester-bomplanter se storie van bevryding.* Tafelberg

Covey, S (1989) *The Seven Habits of Highly Effective People: Powerful lessons in personal change.* Free Press

Egger, SA (2002) *The Killers Among Us: An examination of serial murder and its investigation* (2nd ed). Prentice-Hall

eNCA (16 September 2013) 'Convicted Worcester bomber says sorry' on YouTube, https://www.youtube.com/ watch?v=7QG6FGKbcf0

Federal Bureau of Investigation (2005) *Serial Murder: Multi-disciplinary perspectives for investigators.* Behavioural Analysis Unit-2, National Center for the Analysis of Violent Crime, Critical Incident Response Group, Federal Bureau of Investigation

Feldman Barrett, L (2018) *How Emotions are Made: The secret life of the brain.* Pan Macmillan

Frye, N (2000 [1957]) *Anatomy of Criticism: Four essays.* Princeton University Press

Geberth, VJ (1996) *Practical Homicide Investigation: Tactics, procedures, and forensic techniques* (3rd ed). CRC Press

Geberth, VJ (2003) *Sex-related Homicide and Death Investigation: Practical and clinical perspectives.* CRC Press

Heider, F and Simmel, M (1944) 'An experimental study of apparent behavior' in *The American Journal of Psychology,* 57(2)

Hodgskiss, B (2001) 'A multivariate model of the offence behaviours of South African serial murderers'. Unpublished Master's thesis, Rhodes University

Hodgskiss, B (2004) 'Lessons from serial murder in South Africa' in *Journal of Investigative Psychology and Offender Profiling,* 1(1)

Holmes, RM and DeBurger, J (1988) *Serial Murder.* Sage

Johnson, S (1999) *Who Moved My Cheese?: An amazing way to deal with change in your work and in your life.* Penguin

Kaplan, J, Gimbel, S and Harris, S (2016) 'Neural correlates of maintaining one's political beliefs in the face of counterevidence'. *Scientific Reports* 6, article no 39589

Kaplan, J, Gimbel, S, Dehghani, M, et al (2017) 'Processing narratives concerning protected values: A cross-cultural investigation of neural correlates' in *Cerebral Cortex* 27(2)

Kirk, PT (1953) *Crime Investigation: Physical evidence and the police laboratory.* Interscience Publishers

Labuschagne, GN (2007) 'Serial murder revisited: A psychological exploration of two South African cases'. Doctoral thesis, University of Pretoria

Maruna, S (2000) 'Criminology, desistance and the psychology of the stranger' in D Canter and L Alison (eds), *The Social Psychology of Crime Groups, Teams and networks.* Routledge

Maruna, S (2001) *Making Good: How ex-convicts reform and rebuild their lives.* American Psychological Association

McAdams, DP (1988) *Power, Intimacy and the Life Story: Personological enquiries into identity*. Guilford Press

McAdams, DP (1993) *The Stories We Live By: Personal myths and the making of the self*. William Morrow

McAdams, DP (1995) 'What do we know when we know a person?' in *Journal of Personality*, 63(3)

McAdams, DP (2006) *The Person: A new introduction to personality psychology* (4th ed). Wiley

McAdams, DP (2013). 'The psychological self as actor, agent, and author in *Perspectives on Psychological Science*, 8(3)

McAdams, D (2017) 'The self as a story' on Monmouth College's YouTube channel, https://www.youtube.com/watch?v=ySDUoyL3KHg

McAdams, DP and Cox, KS (2010) 'Self and identity across the life span' in R Lerner, A Freund and M Lamb (eds) *Handbook of Life-span Development*. Wiley

McAdams, DP and McLean, KC (2013). 'Narrative identity' in *Current Directions in Psychological Science*, 22(3)

McAdams, DP, Reynolds, J, Lewis, M et al (2001) 'When bad things turn good and good things turn bad: Sequences of redemption and contamination in life narrative and their relation to psychosocial adaptation in midlife adults and in students' in *Personality and Social Psychology Bulletin* 27(4)

Pennebaker, J (2018) 'Expressive writing in psychological science' in *Perspectives on Psychological Science*, 13(2)

Pennebaker, JW and Beall, SK (1986) 'Confronting a traumatic event: Toward an understanding of inhibition and disease' in *Journal of Abnormal Psychology*, 95(3)

Quinet, K (2011) 'Prostitutes as victims of serial homicide: Trends and case characteristics, 1970–2009' in *Homicide Studies*, 15(1)

Rogers, BA, Chicas, H, Kelly, JM, et al (2023) 'Seeing your life story as a hero's journey increases meaning in life' in *Journal of Personality and Social Psychology*, 125(4)

Royal Museums Greenwich (no date) 'South African star myths' https://www.rmg.co.uk/stories/topics/south-african-star-myths

Salfati, CG, Labuschagne, GN, Horning, AM et al (2015) 'South African serial homicide: Offender and victim demographics and crime scene actions' in *Journal of Investigative Psychology and Offender Profiling*, 12(1)

Saviano, R (transl V Jewiss) (2019) *Gomorrah*. Picador

Seleka, N (4 March 2020) 'Nearly half of the 101 sex workers who died in SA in 2018 and 2019 were murdered' on News24, https://www.news24.com/news24/nearly-half-of-the-101-sex-workers-who-died-in-sa-in-2018-and-2019-were-murdered-20200304

Siegel-Acevedo, D (2021) 'Writing can help us heal from trauma' in *Harvard Business Review*, https://hbr.org/2021/07/writing-can-help-us-heal-from-trauma

Stephens, GJ, Silbert LJ and Hasson, U (2010) 'Speaker–listener neural coupling underlies successful communication' in *The Proceedings of the National Academy of Sciences (PNAS)*, 107(32)

Strydom, J (2020) 'Stefaans Coetzee het bomme geplant, nou plant hy groente' on *Moeilikheid is ons besigheid! met Jaco Strydom*, Apple Podcasts, https://podcasts.apple.com/gb/podcast/moeilikheid-is-ons-besigheid-met-jaco-strydom/id1498398894?i=1000498753742

Terkel, S (1984) *'The Good War': An oral history of World War II*. Pantheon Books

Tonguette, P (2015) 'The Greatest Thing About Studs Terkel was Studs Terkel' in *Humanities* 36(4)

Vetten, L, Jewkes, R, Sigsworth, R, et al (2008) *Tracking Justice: The attrition of rape cases through the criminal justice system in Gauteng*. Tshwaranang Legal Advocacy Centre, the South African Medical Research Council and the Centre for the Study of Violence and Reconciliation

Villman, E (2023) 'Desistance upon release from prison: Narratives of tragedy, irony, romance and comedy' in *The British Journal of Criminology*, 63(5)

White, M (2018) 'Funny moments' on Dulwich Centre Foundation's YouTube channel, https://www.youtube.com/watch?v=TT73fQVvya8

White, RW (1975) *Lives in Progress* (3rd ed). Holt, Rinehart & Winston

About the authors

DR BRIN HODGSKISS was born and raised in Johannesburg. After graduating from Rhodes University with an MA in research psychology, he worked with the South African Police Service before spending 15 years working for the police in the UK. He supported investigations and intelligence work, tackling everything from anti-social behaviour and burglary to terrorism, murder and serial rape. Hodgskiss received his PhD from the University of Pretoria for his exploration of the narratives of serial murderers in South Africa. He has published in international journals, as well as presented academically, on television and radio, on the topic of serial murder. He now works in England's National Health Service and is a freelance consultant in the psychology of storytelling. Hodgskiss lives in Cambridge with his wife, son and greyhound.

NICOLE ENGELBRECHT spent 20 years in corporate management before venturing out into creative entrepreneurship. In 2019, she launched South Africa's first victim-focused true-crime podcast, *True Crime South Africa*. This has grown to become Africa's most successful true-crime podcasts and one of the most listened-to podcasts overall in South Africa. She has also pioneered the true-crime podcast space in collaboration with Showmax in developing the country's first companion podcasts for Showmax's true-crime documentaries. Engelbrecht has published two books, *Samurai Sword Murder: The Morne Harmse Story* and *Sizzlers: The Hate Crime That Tore Sea Point Apart.*